Milt M'Auley

DEDICATION

Ron Webster — trail builder, hike leader, man of the Santa Monica Mountains, and friend — he is this and more. Once in a generation someone comes along at the right time, in the right place, with the talent and energy to get a job done. Ron is that person. Marching to his own drummer, driven by an inner power, with an extraordinary creative ability to visualize and build trails, Ron is making a positive and lasting contribution to public use of the Santa Monica Mountains.

GUIDE

TO THE

BACKBONE

TRAIL

OF THE SANTA MONICA MOUNTAINS

By

MILT McAULEY

ISBN 0-942568-23-0

Library of Congress Card Number 90-83558

Published in the United States of America

Canyon Publishing Company
8561 Eatough Avenue
Canoga Park, CA 91304

Acknowledgements

Without any overstatement of fact the list of people who have contributed significantly to the writing of this book is into the hundreds. Knowing that I do an injustice to most by naming but a few, there is consolation to all that these people, named and un-named, have made great contributions for the preservation of the Santa Monica Mountains. Future generations in centuries to come will have a place to relate directly with nature. Those of you who have endeavored to help bring this about are forever blessed.

HARVEY ANDERSON, who will be 83 years of age in January, 1991, accompanied the State Park team that first laid out the route of the Backbone Trail. His knowledge of the mountains was as invaluable then as it is now. I specially want to thank Harvey for sharing the history of this area with us.

DAVE BROWN. A special note is in order for Dave Brown. He is untiring in his devotion to the Backbone Trail. He is a bulldog when the Santa Monica Mountains are concerned and is and has been a strong force for their preservation. I thank him for the information, maps, and guidance. Future generations will thank him for his untiring devotion to preserving land for their use.

BILL HARRIS, MARY ANN KEEVE, SCOTT McAULEY, AND PADDY CALISTRO. I asked them to read my manuscript and place a red mark at any place they got stopped, or didn't understand something — or became bored. They did this. It helped me a lot. I didn't ask for editing or rewriting. Because I did not always take their advice, don't blame them for things you don't like. I appreciate their participation in the process.

RUTH TAYLOR KILDAY, the fifth generation of her family to be born and raised locally, has devoted the last twelve years exclusively to the Santa Monica Mountains. First working for the National Park Service, then for the Santa Monica Mountains Conservancy, and now as Executive Director of the Mountains Conservancy Foundation, she is a dynamic force in the development and promotion of public use of this land.

LOU LEVY wrote the first book about walking in the Santa Monica Mountains. This has helped promote the understanding and awareness of the natural values of these mountains. The profits from the book are used by the Sierra Club, Santa Monica Mountains Task Force to further their goals.

LINDA PALMER for many years has been the driving force behind the Santa Monica Mountains Trails Council. Linda devotes time and energy working with private and government groups to insure that trail easements are honored, and that those who would make major changes to existing open space provide for trails and wildlife corridors. Linda builds and maintains trails.

BILL HARRIS walked the Backbone Trail using a measuring wheel to refine the distances. We now know that uphill is not farther than downhill on the same trail.

THE SIERRA CLUB SANTA MONICA MOUNTAINS TASK FORCE trail crew has been a capable, independent, motivated, working group since the early 1970s. The crew built more trail by hand in the Santa Monicas than any comparable group. Even though the membership changes over the years, the crew maintains a tradition of service that is unexcelled. I wanted to list the team members, and a sizeable list developed. It became apparent to me that nobody has a complete list of people that have been members of this team. Any list would be incomplete. Rather than offend anyone by omission, and upon the sage advice of several people, we acknowledge all the crew for your outstanding contribution. You know who you are, others know. You are to be commended.

RON WEBSTER has worked at planning, building and maintaining the Backbone Trail system. He inspires others to do the same. He pioneered many routes through the mountains before the trails were laid out. His knowledge of routes and place names has been invaluable for this book.

JIM KENNEY organized and prepared the information on the plant life in the Santa Monica Mountains. He furnished some of the pictures along the trail making it possible for us to "see" what the Backbone Trail is really like.

CONGRESSMAN ANTHONY C. BEILENSON, who as a State Senator was in the vanguard for the preservation of the unique environment features of the Santa Monica Mountains. Later, as a United States Congressman, he introduced the bill resulting in the Santa Monica Mountains Recreation Area. His continued dedication makes the Backbone Trail and other features of our outdoor recreation system possible.

DAN PREECE, Superintendent of the Santa Monica Mountains district of the California Department of Parks and Recreation and his staff have been invaluable in furnishing detailed information about the trail system. I specially thank Greg Nelson.

JOE EDMISTON, Executive Director of the Santa Monica Mountains Conservancy and his staff have furnished me with detailed map information and facilities data.

DAVID GACKENBACH, Superintendent of the Santa Monica Mountains National Recreation Area and his entire staff have furnished information to me. It is often in great detail, so that the trail information will be as accurate as I can get it. I specially thank Vondell Scharrer, Alice Allen, Bonnie Clarfield, Mike Baker, Tom Young and Jean Bray.

We need to make an important statement and observation. The organizations headed by David Gackenbach, Joe Edmiston, and Dan Preece, cooperate and support one another to an outstanding degree. Collectively their "can-do" attitude has performed miracles in the area of planning, acquisition, and use of this land so that we now have a system of Parks. We the public, and future generations, are fortunate to have people such as these dedicating their energies to the Santa Monica Mountains.

PAT MAYLARD, our daughter, for her many hours of help in our final preparation of the book.

Last but certainly not least, my wife Maxine has been a steadying hand throughout. Her keen perception and sound judgement have prevented many an error had I been left to my own devices. Thanks, Macky.

*   *   *

Illustrations on pages 24, 32, 34 and 97 by Janet Solum. Pictures by James P. Kenney as labelled. All others by Milt McAuley.

Cover credits by Milt and Maxine McAuley
    Front: Rock Pool — Malibu Creek State Park 1990
    Back: Santa Ynez Canyon 1980

Preface

The Backbone Trail is still part idea and part reality. The thought of an east-west trail in the Santa Monica Mountains has been around for a long time. It has not always been under the name "Backbone," and not always in its present alignment. The term "Ridge Trail" was common in the late 1960s and early 1970s when a longer trail, one beginning at Griffith Park and ending at Point Mugu, was discussed. The term "Backbone" came into common use about 1974 when two State legislative acts focused on trails. The late state Senator Randolph Collier and the former Assemblyman Barry Keene guided a bill through the Legislature to establish trails connecting state parks. The former Assemblyman Paul Priolo sponsored a funded bill for a trail linking the state parks in the Santa Monica Mountains. Development of the land near Griffith Park made it impractical to obtain a suitable trail along ridges west of Griffith Park. The plan for the trail became the present route: Will Rogers State Historic Park to Point Mugu State Park. In 1979 we received a major setback to the Backbone Trail. The Department of Parks and Recreation concluded that without eminent domain the trail corridor between Topanga State Park and Malibu Creek State Park could not be acquired. In 1981 a bill sponsored by Assemblyman Howard Berman appropriated $6 million for funding to complete the trail link between these two Parks. The Santa Monica Mountains Conservancy, headed by Joe Edmiston, did the spade work and acquired the corridor with the funds. Dave Brown, one of the leaders of the grass roots movement behind the Backbone Trail states in part: ". . . . In retrospect, this was the critical turning point." Indeed it was a critical turning point. The vision began to become reality. Exploratory hikes through the chaparral became frequent, maybe not routine, but feasible.

For 6 years, beginning in 1983, a small group walked (and crawled) the length of the trail, built and unbuilt, on an annual basis. We scheduled 5 to 7 days on alternate Sundays for the event, setting up car shuttles so we could walk the distance in one direction, east to west. Each year's route varied a little because on the unbuilt trail segments, finding the same path through the chaparral is difficult. The walks had some value; after three years, the Park made a decision to build the 6-mile Saddle Peak — Saddle

Creek segment. Early in 1986 Ron Webster and friends laid out the trail with flags. Later we received State Park approval to build.

In the summer of 1987 the Oat Mountain California Conservation Corps (CCC), The Camarillo CCC, and the Los Angeles Conservation Corps built the 3-mile Saddle Creek segment. In 1988 and early 1989 the Sierra Club volunteer crew built the 1½ miles of Piuma Ridge Trail, an important link of the Backbone Trail. During 1989 and 1990 the Sierra Club volunteer crew has been building the 2-mile Saddle Peak segment. (As this book goes to press work still progresses.)

In the Western part of the trail, work is in progress on the connector between Point Mugu State Park and Circle X Ranch, a unit of the National Park Service (NPS). This is a rugged and spectacular segment that comes off Boney Mountain west ridge to Sycamore Canyon. A CCC crew is carving the trail on the west ridge of the mountain.

In 1986 the Youth Conservation Corps completed a segment between Newton Motorway and Latigo Canyon Road. Then again between 1987 and 1989 the Camarillo and Oat Mountain Conservation Crews, Los Angeles Conservation Corps, and the Urban and National Student Conservation Association constructed 2.1 miles of trail between Latigo Canyon Road and Kanan Dume Road. All on National Park Service land. Further work is dependent on obtaining a trail easement on the western end. The trailhead maps on pages 54-58 show details of trail status.

Using the present projected configurations as a guide, my estimate is that the trail will total 65 miles in length.

Of this distance, 32 miles of Backbone Trail existed at the time of land acquisition. When land came into public ownership starting in the late 1960s the state inherited parts of what was to become the Backbone Trail. A route existed from Will Rogers State Historic Park across Topanga State Park to Trippet Ranch. Two routes crossed Malibu Creek State Park. Point Mugu State Park had an extensive trail system. A trail existed on Castro Motorway at the time the NPS acquired Castro Crest. Part, but not all, of the trail across the Circle X Ranch was built in the 1950s under supervision of the Exchange Club (the service organization that founded Circle X). Since the early 1970s, 12 miles of new Backbone Trail have been built (this does not count parallel trails such as Musch Ranch and Backbone Trail/Solstice across Castro Crest). This gives us 43 miles of completed Backbone Trail and about 22 miles of construction remaining.

The work does go on, and with renewed interest and help from potential users we can expect results at an increasing rate.

Table of Contents

Introduction

Welcome to the Backbone Trail — sixty-five miles of mountainous travel from Will Rogers State Historic Park to Point Mugu. Hidden in the mountain ridges and recesses, the trail guides us through woodlands, past waterfalls, over grasslands, and to remote and secluded places. Isolated from civilization, this trail offers adventure, excitement, and the opportunity to observe nature in an almost undisturbed state.

Come walk the trail. You will visit sites of historic value, walk over land once the domain of native American Indians, and explore back-country that few ever see. Witness a variety of environment from meadows of wildflowers to dry chaparral ridges. You may see deer, most certainly the tracks. Red-tailed hawks soar overhead looking for a ground squirrel or rabbit. Scrub jays will scold you for coming through their territory. In a chaparral forest an unseen wrentit will give out a staccato sound somewhat like a ping-pong ball bouncing on a table. Coyotes are rarely seen but often heard just after sundown. Bob-cats patiently stalk dusky-footed woodrats but are seldom seen. A southern pacific rattlesnake will find a warm spot along a trail on cooler days and come out early morning or in the evening on very hot days. Lucky is the person that sees the elusive mountain lion — and even then it's only a glimpse. And yes, you will find a few ticks in spring and summer. After a wet winter, late spring produces a few flies, but generally speaking, insects are not a problem.

So, indulge yourself, come out on the trail for an adventure. Savor the spell that the mountains cast upon you and return home at the end of the day with an aching body but a rested soul.

History

THE INDIANS

The first people coming to the Santa Monica Mountains were Native American Indians. Estimates of their initial arrival are subject to speculation but a date of around 9000 years ago would be acceptable to many people. Some earlier sporadic arrivals could have occurred but positive evidence is sketchy. During the last Ice Age ending 11,500 years ago the oceans were several hundred feet lower than now. Most primitive people lived near the ocean so evidence of early man's occupation, if any, would be under water.

Although not known for sure, the early arrivals were pre-decessors of the Chumash people. Linguistically the Chumash language is related to other languages of central and northern California, yet is uniquely distinctive, showing a separation from other languages for thousands of years. The Chumash themselves, at the time of the Spanish invasion, spoke seven dialects, indicating physical divisions for a long period.

About 7000 years ago small village sites were located on the coast near freshwater streams in grassland and coastal sage scrub plant communities. Food sources were mainly hard seeds available most of the year. Walnut, toyon, and holly-leaf cherry were available during fall and winter.

About 5000 years ago the processing of acorns for food became known. Previously the bitter tannic acid in acorns made this food source inedible. When pounding in mortars and leaching with water was discovered, this new source of a plentiful food changed the Indian's life. Population increased and village sites expanded in size and number. Inland villages became permanent.

A gradual thousand-year-long transition began from dependence on seed gathering to a subsistence system that included permanent settlements having temporary hunting and foraging camps. Hunting and fishing increased, fishhooks were developed, and a new pattern of coastal villages evolved. About 2300 years ago the village

13

distribution stabilized and remained constant until the time of the Spanish invasion. For 2000 years a continued cultural evolution included the development of large spear points, an increased emphasis on hunting and seafood, and shell ornaments.

Around 1500 years ago the Chumash culture emerged. Social structure changes included main villages, each supporting several smaller living sites away from the main village. Members of the complex were allocated foraging areas. These changes intensified the exploitation of food sources. Land ownership was recognized, first as village-owned and later as family-owned.

The Chumash traded goods with their neighbors, the bow and arrow was discovered, the evolution of mortars and pestles made them more efficient. Fused shale was discovered resulting in its use for projectile points.

At the time of the Spanish invasion in 1769 technical accomplishments of the Chumash were noted. Planked canoes, a serviceable economic system, a well-developed political structure, and a concept of order in their universe were standard.

Evidence shows that about 3000 years ago Shoshonean speaking people moved into the Los Angeles basin, displacing the people there. At the time of Spanish arrival Chumash lived west of the ridge dividing Malibu and Topanga canyons. The Shoshonean speaking people lived east. When Portolá arrived in 1769 he found a viable thriving people whose culture had adjusted to their environment. Their progress in government, religion, and relations with their neighbors was positive.

This was about to change.

THE SPANISH

The defeat of the Aztec empire by the Spanish under Hernán Cortéz in 1521 began a rapid occupation of Mexico. Juan Rodriguez Cabrillo arrived off the coast of the Santa Monica Mountains in 1542 to be greeted by friendly Indians on October 10. He honored them by coming ashore and claiming their land in the name of Spain. With some regularity, Spanish ships on the trade route from the Philippines to Mexico passed by the Santa Monica Mountains, and Sebastian Vizcaino sailed the coast in 1602. Spain ignored California until 1769, when Gaspar de Portolá made his first historic trip north. The party crossed the Santa Monica Mountains through

Sepulveda Pass and continued across the San Fernando Valley to Castaic, turning west to follow the Santa Clara River to Ventura.

The Portolá expedition consisted of Gaspar de Portolá, one navigator, two priests, 49 mounted soldiers, and 15 Indians. Mules carried the supplies.

On the return trip after searching for Monterey Bay, Portolá came inland along the northern foothills of the Santa Monica Mountains. He crossed over Cahuenga Pass on an Indian trail — now the Hollywood Freeway. In short order the missionization of the Indians began. Missions were built by Indian labor, and the Indians left their traditional life style to live at the missions. The Indians suffered mass deaths because of introduced diseases. They lost their land, their culture, and their dignity. Now, two hundred years later, the value of this loss is slowly being realized. We can all recognize and cherish the culture that barely survived.

During the Spanish expansion of California the town of Los Angeles was founded on 4 September 1781 by 11 families and four soldiers totalling 48 people. They travelled for seven months from the mining town of Los Alamos, Sonora Mexico, having been recruited from nearby villages. The name of the town has been shortened from "El Puebla de Nuestra Señora la Reina de Los Angeles de Porciúncula," or the town of "Our Lady Queen of the Angels of Porciúncula."

THE MEXICANS

Mexico declared independence from Spain in 1821. The Church lost political domination and its vast land holdings. The Mexican colonization law of 1824 and the supplimentary Reglamento of 1828 were passed. Land grants were made. By 1834 civil control was no longer in religious hands. The missions functioned as religious institutions but lost control of the large agricultural and ranch industries.

Many times various factions have tried to divide California, north from south. The first division of record is immediately after the Portolá expedition of 1769. An ecclesiastical partition of California granted the Dominicans authority in Baja and the Franciscans in Alta California. The original line was drawn west from the head of the Gulf of California to the ocean. The dividing line moved north as the Spanish influence moved north.

15

A year after Mexico gained independence from Spain in 1821 the government in Mexico City proposed to divide the State. In 1831 the division became fact when northern and southern factions began fighting. A division was made that lasted 18 months. Of interest to the Backbone Trail hiker is that the dividing line between "south" and "north" California was along the east-west crest of the Santa Monica Mountains, about where the Backbone Trail is located. The Rancho era itself was of short duration because the Mexican-American War of 1846-1848 ended with California becoming United States territory.

THE AMERICANS

Under the later years of Spain's rule and throughout Mexico's ownership of California, foreigners came to stay. First, mountain men, explorers and in the early 1840s immigrant parties. John C. Fremont led a military force into California in 1845 (collecting plant specimens). Fremont was on location when the Mexican-American war began in 1846. He signed the peace treaty along with General Pico for Mexico at Campo de Cahuenga on 13 January 1847. A copy of the treaty in Spanish, and an English translation, is displayed at Los Encinos State Historic Park. The official ending of the war took place more than a year later at Guadalupe Hidalgo on 2 February 1848.

I'll shorten the history by skipping the events that have taken California to a State with nearly 30 million people and the need for open space wherever we can preserve it. The building of roads, homes, gas pipelines, garbage dumps, water pipelines, power lines, telephone lines, recreation areas, parks, hiking trails, bicycle trails, wheelchair trails, Braille trails, equestrian trails, and the need to preserve the hundreds of archaeological sites that have survived thousands of years — all place a great strain on the mountains and those who must plan to provide for all.

Natural History

In the future, many people will walk or ride the Backbone Trail. Some for the exercise, some for camaraderie, and some because of an interest in plants, animals, geology or history. Usually some combination of interests will call us to the trail. A basic understanding of the natural history found in these mountains could add much to the visit.

WEATHER

The climate of the Santa Monica Mountains is normally of cool, wet winters and hot, dry summers. Four other places in the world have similar climate: the Mediterranean region, central Chile (near Santiago), southwestern Australia (near Perth), and the cape region of South Africa. The term "Mediterranean climate" is applied to these regions.

Coastal Southern California and Baja share similar climate with four other parts of the world.

This type of climate occurs about 33° latitude on western edges of continents. The angle of inclination of the earth's axis with respect to its orbit around the sun causes intense summer heat in these areas, and allows for cool but not cold winters.

The weather conditions in the Santa Monica Mountains are important because the vegetation cycle differs from the "customary" idea of plant growth. Here because of pronounced summer droughts the growing season begins in the fall with winter rains and continues into spring. Chaparral has adapted to this cycle by having small thick leaves, which are often hairy to prevent evaporation of moisture. Many plants are annual so seeds that mature in the spring will lie dormant during the hot summer. Most plants recover from a fire.

A semipermanent high pressure cell over our part of the Pacific Ocean between 30° and 40° north latitude deflects many storms from southern California. Sometimes the Pacific High is weakened or displaced, and storms, which form in the Gulf of Alaska, come through southern California. Once the High is displaced we can expect a week or more of wet weather until the high pressure area is restored. This means we have hot, dry summers and sometimes rain in the winter.

TOPOGRAPHY

The Santa Monica Mountains are an east-west trending, steep ridged, isolated range. Located in southern California in Los Angeles and Ventura counties, the range is bounded on the south by the Los Angeles basin and the Pacific Ocean. San Fernando Valley, the Conejo Valley, and the Oxnard Plain are to the north. West to east from Point Mugu to Griffith Park is 46 miles. Sandstone Peak (which is volcanic) at 3111 feet is the highest point of the mountains. The Pacific Ocean shoreline is the lowest point. Streams originating south of the crest flow south to the ocean. Streams originating north of the crest flow north, with one exception: Malibu Creek cuts through the mountains. Malibu Creek drains much of the central mountains using its main tributaries Medea Creek and Triunfo Creek. The Los Angeles River (now concrete lined) is the main waterway for the San Fernando Valley Streams. The Los Angeles River flows around the east end of the mountains and goes south entering the ocean at Long Beach.

Calleguas Creek drains the northern slope of the western part of the mountains.

A network of highways and roads make the trailheads accessible. As a general rule motor vehicles are allowed on paved roads but are not allowed on dirt roads. An exception is the open eight mile unpaved section of Mulholland Drive.

A system of trails following ridges and natural stream courses connect together so that much of the parkland is available. The Backbone Trail is designed so that these connector trails will lead the traveller from one end of the mountains to the other and occasionally access the ocean to the south and the valleys to the north.

PLANT LIFE

Vegetation is a vital natural resource of the area. It is also home for insects and animals. It stabilizes the soil from erosion by providing a screen from rain and by dropping layers of leaves. Root systems hold the soil in place and retain moisture. Plants are the basis of the food chain for the entire animal community. Even after a fire, nutrients in the form of ash and charcoal provide a seedbed for the next generation of vegetation. Seeds having survived a fire, and in some cases need a fire, sprout and perpetuate the species. Tested over several million years the plants that have adapted to a hot, dry summer, a winter growing season, and periodic fire are the plants growing in the mountains now. The plants that once were here, but did not adapt, are absent.

Botanists are not all in agreement on the nomenclature of the plant communities of the mountains. The authoritative book, *Flora of the Santa Monica Mountains, California* by Raven, Thompson, and Prigge describes 12 plant communities. Larger lists have been suggested and depending upon interpretation of a community, may be valid. I will list and describe eight in this book because the Backbone Trail doesn't cross all communities. Also, I've added a couple because my belief is that some communities (such as a solid cactus patch), even though normally listed in more inclusive descriptions, are distinct and worth separate treatment. I recommend that for a complete and accurate treatment of the subject you refer to the book by Raven, Thompson, and Prigge. The eight plant communities described on the following pages are:

19

(1) Chaparral, (2) Southern Oak Woodland, (3) Coastal Sage Scrub, (4) Riparian Woodland, (5) Valley Grassland, (6) Cactus Scrub, (7) Cliffside, and (8) Freshwater Marsh.

CHAPARRAL

This community dominates the Santa Monica Mountain vegetation. High rocky ridges, steep slopes, and poor soil are required environments for chaparral. A small amount of rainfall, all of which falls during winter, is necessary for its survival. Periodic fires are essential for chaparral to regenerate indefinitely. During normal growth manzanita, ceanothus, chamise and others deposit toxins on the soil, thereby inhibiting the sprouting of seeds — even their own. In time the forest ages and dies. Fire is required to remove the dead wood, volatize the soil toxins, and deposit nutrients for new growth. Characteristic plants are: ceanothus, chamise, red shanks, manzanita, mountain mahogany, toyon, bush poppy, scrub oak, and laurel sumac.

Hikers on the Backbone Trail in Circle X Ranch.
Chaparral on both sides.

SOUTHERN OAK WOODLAND

Deep soil in sheltered areas is often the environment of southern oak woodlands. Found more often on north facing slopes than on sunnier exposures, and above intermittent streams, the woodlands dominate extensive areas. The Backbone Trail goes through southern oak woodlands in the Topanga watershed, lower levels of the Malibu watershed, extensive slopes of Zuma and Trancas canyons, and in random locations of Point Mugu State Park. Some characteristic plants are: coast live oak, bay, walnut, canyon sunflower, woodfern, bush monkeyflower, poison oak, and toyon.

Southern oak woodland in Trancas Canyon

COASTAL SAGE SCRUB

Aptly named, this plant community is usually facing the coast but significant stands can be found inland. The term "scrub" is used here to define a shrub, particularly with many branches low on the plant. Sage and sagebrush are normally the dominant plants. Generally with shallower root systems and less densely spaced than chaparral, coastal sage scrub grows at lower elevations and in areas of less rainfall. Characteristic plants are black, purple, and white sage, California sagebrush, buckwheat, goldenbush, sumac, and bush sunflower.

James P. Kenney

Coastal sage scrub on hillside above Sycamore Canyon

22

RIPARIAN WOODLAND

Riparian comes from a Latin word meaning river and this plant community is found along streams as well as near lakes and reservoirs. All streams need not be perennial to support the community and in fact differences in the amount of soil moisture will determine the plant species. Many streams go dry in summer but retain a subterranean moisture layer a few feet down. Characteristically flooded areas support willows, white alder, horsetail, creek and scarlet monkeyflower, and speedwell. On the bank away from the water yet in the zone, we can find cottonwood, bigleaf maple, stream orchid, sycamore, blackberry, poison oak, and mulefat.

Willows line both sides of Malibu Creek upstream of Century Lake.

VALLEY GRASSLAND

Grasslands that had remained more or less constant for thousands of years have been permanently altered by the introduction of alien species. Less than half of the 100 grass species are native, a quarter of the sunflowers are introduced and complete fields of black mustard are introduced. However, most of the grasslands still present have been grasslands for a long time. Aside from the many species of grass the community is characterized by sunflowers, mustards, mariposa lilies, blue-eyed grass, lupines, and filaree.

La Jolla Valley Grassland
(Boney Mountain is on the eastern horizon)

CACTUS SCRUB

Occasionally cactus plants will cover an area to the exclusion of all other plants, at which time it becomes a unique community. Normally individual cactus plants are dispersed in a coastal sage scrub community and are just one of many contributing plants. A pure stand of cactus plants is haven for rabbits, squirrels, and maybe a snake or two. The rabbits and squirrels keep other plants from growing, and by foraging the perimeter allow the cactus patch to grow. The community provides haven for the rodents so that hawks and coyotes can't get them when among the cactus patch. Only prickly pear cactus form plant communities in the Santa Monica Mountains. Neither beavertail or cholla cacti grow close enough to exclude other plants.

CLIFFSIDE

Some plants grow only on cliffs. Most plants are unable to survive in the absence of soil, the lack of a reliable source of water, and the exposure. Cliffs usually are isolated structures surrounded by some other community, and the same plant species are often found growing on the rocks regardless of the surrounding community. (Hawkweed grows along Castro motorway on a high, dry ridge surrounded by chaparral and also on a cliff in Cold Creek Canyon near a southern oak woodland.) Although these plants are found elsewhere, look for the following on cliffs, roadcuts, or among the rocks at the base: dudleya, spike moss, golden yarrow, Tejon Milk-aster, shrubby bedstraw, fuchsia, and Santa Susana tarweed.

FRESHWATER MARSH

Standing water along the shore of ponds, slow moving streams, and moist soil will support this plant community. Characteristic species are cat-tail, pond lily, rush, water-cress, knotweed, and yellow water-weed.

ANIMAL LIFE

The wildlife of the Santa Monica Mountains along the Backbone Trail makes every effort to remain hidden — and with just cause. People, dogs and cats have encroached upon the terrain of the native animals and caused severe losses. The last giant California condor soared overhead and made a dive down into a canyon in 1937; bears no longer range their 100 square mile territory (thank goodness); and even the California mule deer is hard to find in some areas. The urban dream continues to take its toll; but if you walk into the mountains often enough, you are bound to find wildlife.

California quail are found in the fringe area between chaparral and riparian woodland as well as in coastal sage. Sometimes they are found near homes, especially when water is available. Deer are full of surprises. We will see them crossing the trail during mid-day, as a silhouette at night on a ridge, and as a flash up from a stream that we might be walking along. Seldom seen, but often heard, is the kr-r-r-eck-ck of the Pacific tree frog. Most intermittent streams and even small temporary ponds are places to look and listen.

Swallow-tail
Butterfly

Turtle

Top —   Lizard

Left -   Rattlesnake

Rt. —   Tarantula (on Jean
          Dillingham's hand)

27

The coast horned lizard is often seen in the fringe area of the chaparral. This 3-to 4-inch long, flat, wide lizard is active during the daytime and will be seen in rocky, sandy, or gravelly places. It can change color from a dark to a light phase in only a few minutes and often closely matches the color of the background. This refugee from prehistoric times looks ferocious, but is really tame. This lizard feeds on insects, including bees. Beekeepers who place hives near the chaparral have reported that occasionally a horned lizard will take up a station near a hive entrance and grab a bee now and then.

A coast horned lizard blends into the background.

Four kinds of salamanders live in the Santa Monica Mountains: the arboreal salamander, the California slender salamander, Eschscholtz's salamander, and the California newt.

The California newt lives on land most of its life but returns to water to breed. The migration to water usually occurs in winter and spring during or after a rain. The eggs are attached to rocks, sticks, or other objects in the water, and hatch 5-10 weeks later. The California newt spends its larval state in the water, usually a coastal stream. Transformation takes place late in the summer and the young newt leaves the water and hides in damp areas nearby.

California Newt

The other three salamanders are terrestrial through all phases of life. During the dry part of the year they stay under rocks, in burrows in the ground, or other subterranean retreats that afford some protection from becoming dry. When the ground becomes wet from the winter and spring rains these salamanders emerge and may be found under leaf litter and other surface material. Courtship and breeding may occur anytime that they are out on the surface. The California slender salamander lays eggs in late fall and winter, with hatching in the spring. The eggs are deposited under rocks and other underground places. The arboreal salamander deposits eggs in rotten logs or hollows in trees in late spring or early summer. Hatching takes place in fall and early winter. The eggs of the Eschscholtz's salamander are usually deposited underground. The young of all three terrestrial salamanders hatch as miniature adults, the transformation from larvae having taken place in the egg.

You will seldom see, but often note, the presence of coyotes in the mountains. If you are high on a ridge at evening you may hear the staccato yipping and then howling down in a valley; if you are in the valley they will likely be on the ridge. Also watch underfoot. Coyote "scat," characteristically containing the big holly-leaf cherry seeds will often be deposited right on the trail. There

29

is no modesty about coyotes; they find an open spot away from trees and bushes, usually in the middle of the trail, and make their deposit.   Fortunately this insures the optimum condition for the holly-leaf cherry seed to sprout, processed whole through the intestinal tract, placed in an open, sunny spot and provided with its own fertilizer!   October ends the holly-leaf cherry season and the toyon season begins for the coyote.   Walnuts, acorns, and laurel seeds are not on the coyote diet.

The Southern Pacific rattlesnake is an important resident of the Santa Monica Mountains.   They are seen often enough that it is prudent to be aware of their characteristics.   Because they are unable to control body temperature as mammals do, they seek an area in their temperature range between 64° and 89° F., with a preference for the mid 80s.   This means that during the heat of the day in summer the rattlesnake will find shade and wait for late afternoon or evening to move around.   They hibernate in the winter, coming out in early spring, and are then likely to be seen during the day.

Most snakes stay in an area for their lifetime rather than traveling great distances.   Over a period of months it is not likely that a snake will travel very far from home, with some exceptions.

Breeding usually takes place during March or April with the young being born alive 6 months later.   A brood of 11 is average. The recognition of a sexually receptive female by an active male appears to be by sight and smell.   Some snakes have a 2-year reproductive cycle, the ripe female copulating in the fall and ovulating the following spring.

The mating act as witnessed by a group of us on one occasion, involved an entwining in slow but constant twisting and swaying motion.   The heads and about 1/3 of the bodies were off the ground.   A hiking group out on Sullivan Ridge came upon two mating rattlers about 9:30 p.m. on 16 August.   Both snakes were rattling rather gently and did not appear to change their activity, nor seem to be threatened by the presence of people shining flashlights.

Rattlesnakes sense the presence of warm animals by heat sensitive pits that are located below and forward of each eye.   Good depth perception in locating prey is important because most foraging is done when visibility is poor at dusk or after dark.

Rattlesnakes do not hear in the normal sense.   They probably detect ground-borne vibrations through their body or head if in contact with the ground, but do not hear air-borne vibrations. Rather unique, but they don't "hear" their own rattle.

Smelling is done in a pair of spherical chambers in the roof of the mouth. The forked tongue flicks out, picks up odorous particles from the air and transfers these samples to the chambers where sensory cells transmit the information to the brain.

To conclude this segment on the rattlesnake, it can be noted that the pupil of the eye is vertically elliptical and that the pupil of all other Santa Monica Mountain snakes is round. If you are close enough to note this difference, you are TOO CLOSE.

Rattlesnake swallowing a woodrat.
(The rattlesnake was in the process of swallowing the woodrat when I took the picture. My next shot was to be a close-up — about 12 inches away. Quickly, the woodrat was free, the snake was coiling, and I was scooting backwards on my stomach.)

Red-tailed
Hawk

Bobcat

Coyote

Cottontail

Mule
Deer

Mountain
Lion

Gray
Fox

Calif
Ground
Squirrel

32

Left

Ron Webster

Planning the route of the Saddle Creek segment of the Backbone Trail.

Below

Harvey Anderson clears trails with a bush hook.

View of the Saddle Peak Trail, eastbound near the top.

Mendenhall Oak 8/24/1982   before the Dayton Canyon fire and on 10/2/1982 after the fire.

Geology

The Pacific Plate — the part of the earth's crust under the Pacific Ocean and as far inland as the San Andreas Fault — has been slowly moving against the North American Plate. This action is a major cause of mountain building in California. The land was forced up to become the Santa Monica Mountains less than 10 million years ago. Most of the geologic history prior to then happened as sedimentary deposits on the ocean floor. Land rose above the ocean on several previous occasions and later subsided. Volcanic activity resulted in massive igneous intrusions about 16-12 million years ago (mya), but for the most part that activity was below the bottom of the ocean and only occasionally broke through to the top of the sedimentary layer.

Although nowhere exposed, the 200-million-year-old ocean floor — the crustal section of the Pacific Plate — is the oldest formation in the Santa Monica Mountains. Santa Monica Slate, the first sedimentary deposit, was laid down in a shallow sea during the Jurassic Period, 190-135 mya. Santa Monica Slate is found in roadcuts in Sepulveda Pass and as far west as Sullivan and Rustic Canyons where outstanding examples may be seen. Going west on Rogers Road we will be walking on Santa Monica Slate the last 1½ miles until we come to the Temescal fireroad junction. During late Jurassic and early Cretaceous Periods (about 135 mya) granite intruded into the slate.

The Tuna Canyon Formation, an Upper Cretaceous, 135-70 mya, marine sediment of sandstone, siltstone, and conglomerate, overlies the Santa Monica Slate. The land rose above the ocean during several significant periods of time, only to subside again. One such time occurred in the Early Paleocene Epoch, 70 mya, when the Simi Formation nonmarine conglomerate was deposited. This layer, characterized by rounded cobbles and boulders of quartzite, granitic, rhyolitic and gneissic rocks, is limited in its occurrence — the best known exposure is in Upper Solstice Canyon on private property.

Later, during Lower Paleocene and Eocene times, 60-50 mya, a fossil bearing marine layer of pebbly conglomerate, sandstone, and siltstone was deposited on the Tuna Canyon Formation. Examples of this Coal Canyon Formation are found in Carbon (formerly Coal) Canyon.

The Llajas (?) Formation is a marine sequence of sandstone, siltstone, and pebbly conglomerate that overlies the Coal Canyon Formation in a few places in the Santa Monica Mountains. A well exposed 1300-foot thick section of this Eocene, 50-40 mya, formation is seen in upper Solstice Canyon along part of the trail that goes west from the parking lot at the end of Corral Canyon Road.

During the late Eocene, Oligocene, and early Miocene times, 40-25 mya, the land again rose above the ocean and the nonmarine Sespe Formation of pebbly sandstone, mudstone, and coarse grained sandstone was laid down in flood plains. The Backbone Trail is on Sespe Formation for several miles as the trail traverses the ridge at the head of Corral Canyon and Solstice Canyon. Backbone Trail/ Castro winds through the tilted ridges of rock. The east mile of Backbone Trail/Solstice is also on Sespe Formation.

The marine Vaqueros Formation containing shellfish fossils, characteristically *Turritella Inezana,* overlays the Sespe. This fine-grained sandy siltstone, mudstone, medium-to coarse-grained well-sorted formation was deposited during the Lower Miocene Epoch, 25-20 mya. Upper Trancas Canyon is one of many places to find this rock. The Backbone Trail has not been built in Trancas, but an access does exist from Encinal Canyon Road.

The Topanga Group is a Middle Miocene, 20-12 mya, sequence of sedimentary and volcanic rocks totalling about 18,000 feet in thickness. It is divided into three formations: a lower formation of sedimentary rock (Topanga Canyon Formation), a middle formation of volcanic rock (Conejo Volcanics) and an upper formation of sedimentary rock (Calabasas Formation) that interlayers with and overlies the volcanic. Examples of Topanga Group formations are widespread and common. A well-known collecting area for a variety of molluscan fauna is from the Topanga Canyon Formation along Old Topanga Canyon Road. The Conejo Volcanics are widespread in the central and western part of the mountains. Good examples are Goat Buttes in Malibu Creek State Park, but many other volcanic rocks are found throughout. The Calabasas Formation is a thick wide-spread sequence of sandstone, siltstone, and breccia. It receives its name from an exposure in Stokes Canyon about 2 miles west of Calabasas Peak. (The rock on Calabasas Peak is the Topanga Canyon Formation.)

The Modelo Formation was laid down during the late Miocene and early Pliocene Epochs, 12-8 mya, when the land was under a deep sea. Diatomaceous shale, siltstone, shale, and sandstone overlies the Topanga Group. The north slope of the central part of the mountains is made up of Modelo shale. Good examples can be seen in the roadcuts along Topanga Canyon Boulevard south of Mulholland Drive to the summit and one-third mile beyond. I have not seen any Modelo Shale on the Backbone Trail.

The Malibu Coast Fault runs east-west from the mouth of Carbon Canyon to Leo Carrillo Beach. South of the fault the sequence of rock differs from that found in the rest of the Santa Monica Mountains. A 4000-foot exploratory well drilled near Point Dume determined the sequence, starting with the oldest rock: Catalina Schist, Trancas Formation, Zuma Volcanics, and Monterey Shale.

Catalina Schist of late Mesozoic Era is the underlying formation, and is not found anywhere on the surface.

The Trancas Formation is sandstone, mudstone, shale, claystone, and breccia of the early and middle Miocene epoch, 25-15 mya. Zuma Volcanic is of about the same age and interbedded with the sedimentary Trancas Formation. Neither formation is exposed at their base, and most of the information regarding thickness comes from core samples from oil well drilling.

Monterey Shale is of middle and late Miocene ages, 18-11 mya, of marine clay shale that is variably diatomaceous, bituminous, siliceous, and sandy. Dolomite and chert are common. The formation is about 3000 feet thick at Point Dume. Much of the area is overlain by marine terrace deposits of upper Pleistocene age, three mya and less.

GEOLOGIC COLUMN - SOUTH OF MALIBU COAST FAULT

Era	Periods / Epochs	Time in million years	Formation	Where to find examples
Quarternary			Terrace deposits	On the Point Dume plateau
	Pleistocene			N. of PCH in the Zuma Beach Area
		3		
Tertiary				
	Pliocene			
		11		
			Monterey Shale	Point Dume Cliffs on inland side of PCH along Zuma Beach
		18		
	Miocene		Zuma Volcanics	Point Dume
			Trancas	N of PCH in Trancas Cyn Area
		25		
				Missing
		70		
				Missing
		100		
			Catalina Schist	Not exposed

GEOLOGIC COLUMN - SANTA MONICA MOUNTAINS

Eras	Periods / Epochs	Time in million years	Event or formation	Where to find examples
	Quarternary		Continued mountain building	
	Holocene			
		0.01		
	Pleistocene		Faulting Erosion	Everywhere
		3		
	Tertiary		Mountain Building	
	Pliocene			
		11		
			Modelo	North slope of Mts
			Topanga SS	Calabasas Pk
	Miocene		Conejo Volc.	Mulholland HWY NW of Calab. Pk
			Vaqueros	Upper Trancas Cyn East Topanga F.R.
		25		
	Oligocene		Sespe	Upper Solstice Cyn
		40		
			Llajas	Upper Solstice Cyn Carbon Cyn
	Eocene			
		60	Coal Cyn	Los Flores Cyn
	Paleocene		Simi Congl.	Upper Solstice Cyn
		70		
				Garapito Cyn
	Cretaceous		Tuna Cyn	Pena/Tuna Cyn
		135	Granite	Griffith Park
	Jurassic		Santa	Rustic Cyn
			Monica	Sullivan Cyn
			180Slate	Sepulveda Cyn
	Triassic		200 Floor of the ocean	

39

The Local Environment
and Its Hazards

The local mountains have been in place for several million years. During this time evolutionary processes have brought about a wilderness with a mix of plants and animals in some state of balance. When the Native American Indians came on the scene starting about 9000 years ago, the larger animals (bison and mammoth) were fast disappearing. After the Spaniards arrived grizzly bears were gone. Under our intrusion open space has diminished and animal travel corridors have been shut off. We have also introduced plants that will forever be a bane. We can look forward to the introduction of Lyme disease, a tick borne ailment affecting most animals. This could occur by an infected animal (dog or human) from an area already contaminated. At one time I drank water found in the mountains. I now suspect all water to be contaminated.

Nevertheless our mountains are still wild country. Because they are surrounded by civilization we cannot overlook the remote environment once we are on the trail. One is probably safer than downtown but still some unique hazards are there.

TRAILS

Many trails are fireroads, wide enough for multiple use and well maintained. Some trails are narrow, steep and neglected. One, the Chumash Trail, gains 886 feet in about one-half mile without switchbacks, grading or any of the other niceties. It could be one of the oldest trails in the world, having been in continuous use for about 7000 years. Already, groups have suggested the building of a "real" trail on the slope. I hope they never succeed — the Chumash Trail should be left as it is and kept as a treasure.

Most trails are somewhere between the two extremes, wide enough for groups to pass and at an incline of 10° or less. The Backbone Trail usually fits this criterium. No one can predict the future condition of trails. Rain can wash out sections. Equestrian use after hard rains has caused considerable damage to tread. Chaparral tends to fill in a void so constant maintenance is needed on some trails. Occasionally a tree will fall across a trail. The management agencies of the Backbone Trail have effective maintenance crews and volunteers also do a lot of work, but travellers must expect some inconveniences.

FIRE

Fire can burn a hillside faster than anyone can run. Our Mediterranean climate allows a hot dry summer that develops into a fire danger season every year. Fire closures are posted during extreme danger, and of course if fire is raging keep out of the mountains. Most of the fires are caused by man. Those of us who travel the trails should not be part of the problem.

Fire: 23 October 1978   Temescal Canyon

WATER

Because we do not get much rain, the problem of flooding rarely occurs. Flooding roads, mudslides, and overflowing streams are serious whenever there are extremely heavy rains. Rocks roll down the cliffs of the mountain roads. Pacific Coast Highway can be blocked, sometimes for days. If it rains hard, keep out of the mountains.

SUN

The name Backbone Trail is valid — much of the trail is on exposed ridges. Even at best chaparral is not high enough to give shade. (And to continue the description — chaparral is too high to see over and too dense to get through.) Wear appropriate clothing, especially a hat.

TEMPERATURE

Sun and temperature are usually related but not always so. High temperature can cause discomfort even in shade. Loss of body fluids through perspiration can cause dehydration and concurrent loss of energy. Prevent the condition by drinking water before becoming thirsty. Moderately warm to cool water quenches my thirst better than ice water. For better digestion, stop drinking water one-half hour before lunch.

Two heat induced ailments are heat exhaustion and heat stroke. Heat exhaustion follows heavy perspiration during exertion. It could occur without exertion. Symptoms: feeling tired, faint, moist skin, headache and possible nausea. The skin may be pale. Body temperature is normal, pulse is fast and feeble. Find a cool place, lie down, loosen your clothing, prop your feet up and drink water or fruit juices.

Heat stroke is identified by restlessness and confusion, sometimes unconsciousness. The skin is hot and red and becomes dry. Pulse is fast and strong, body temperature is above normal. Treatment consists of rest in a cool place. Sponge the body with water to reduce the temperature. Get medical help, the condition is serious.

PLANT LIFE

Some plants are toxic when ingested, others cause skin rashes. Avoid eating any plant of which you are not sure. The seeds and all other parts of poison hemlock are deadly. Two seeds of a castor-bean plant will put a person in the hospital. I have an article from the L.A. Times telling of a lady who accidently got some tree-tobacco leaves in a wild-plant salad she made for three friends. All four were hospitalized — the hostess died.

Poison oak, some of the phacelias, nettles, and other plants cause skin rashes.

Stinging nettle

Poison Oak

43

ANIMALS

The earliest I've seen a rattlesnake come out of winter hibernation was on January 31. Some years they don't go into hibernation until December. The rest of the year, be alert. A rattlesnake will avoid a confrontation whenever possible but don't step on one or try to grab him. On hot summer days they look for shade and come out to hunt in the evening or early morning. On cooler days they look for a warm place in the sun.

It is important to watch where you step and avoid probing around rocks or large holes in rocks. Exercise caution when entering a cave or rock shelter on a hot day.

If I owned a dog he would stay home when I hiked. On two occasions I've been able to get a dog away from a rattler before his curiosity caused him trouble. Coyotes avoid being bitten; dogs don't.

Several snakebite treatments are recommended. In the Santa Monica Mountains where medical help is reasonably near I would remain calm; lay the person down; wipe venom away from the puncture areas; wash with soap and water; pat dry; and apply a clean dressing. Carry the person to the nearest emergency room. Do not let the patient exercise.

Even young rattlesnakes are venomous. Also, they are difficult to see. (I got my penny back later.)

Avoid all small animals: ground squirrels, rabbits, mice, etc., alive or dead. You don't want their fleas.

Most animals avoid contact with people so they are not a problem. The large ones — deer, coyote, mountain lion — rarely stay around long enough to be seen.

Because of the dry summers, insects are not the problem they are in wet areas. Deer flies bite in late spring. Some unidentified insects get me around the ankles, so when I plan to get off trail I spray a repellant on my socks. California harvester ants live in the ground, bringing buckwheat seeds into the nest and carry the chaff out, making a ring around the entrance. The ants are a rust-red color, foraging all day except noon. Don't stand around long because they bite without much provocation.

Ticks climb to the tips of blades of grass or brush and wave their eight legs when disturbed, thus attaching to an unsuspecting host. Spring is their active season but it's possible to find a tick anytime. If a tick becomes attached, use tweezers or your thumb and finger to exert a steady pull. This procedure usually works. You might try a counterclockwise twist of one revolution as you pull. A tick that has begun to swell may need the added encouragement of a drop of oil or sun cream to stop his respiration. In ten or fifteen minutes to a half hour, removal becomes easier. If mouth parts break off it will probably infect and come out in a couple of days. See a physician if you become ill or if red swelling appears.

Avoid large piles of sticks and twigs, likely a Woodrat den. Woodrat dens are above ground and are their home. Cone-nose bugs can live in the den. Their bite can cause a serious allergic reaction in sensitive persons.

How To Use
The Guide

The book is written so that one should be able to pick up the guide, find the section of trail, locate the trailhead map and instructions, and know what to expect in the way of mileage, elevation and terrain.

In order to verify this information several of us, notably Bill Harris and I, walked the trail during the summer of 1990. We measured the distance in miles with a wheel. Elevation changes were taken by using the 7½ minute topographic maps of the Santa Monica Mountains. Terrain conditions were obvious and subject to change.

We made an attempt to get the mileages accurate. Our measurement by wheel was to .01 mile and we expected a 1% error. These distances were rounded off to the nearest .1 mile. None of the distances were converted to the metric system. Fifteen or twenty years ago someone was posting both miles and kilometers on our local trails. Whoever did this had a mathematics problem, confusing the two systems. This experience leads me to conclude that distance should be listed in one system only. If anyone wants to convert to kilometers, merely divide my miles by 0.62137 and you will be close.

The measuring wheel doesn't record when it moves slower than two mph. I must admit that a time or two going uphill I slowed down. We measured one trail three times before the mileage looked correct. Anytime the uphill mileage was less than the downhill mileage, something was wrong. Uphill is always farther than downhill, isn't it? On the uncompleted part of the Saddle Peak Trail we carried the wheel and paced the distance. We independently came close enough to agree on the distance. On the trail segments to be built in the future, I have merely guessed the distance based upon the map measured mileage modified by elevation change. The missing information will of necessity wait correction until trail completion.

The Backbone Trail is on land managed by different agencies and as a result the rules and regulations may vary. These agencies post rules and regulations and are available as handout information at rangers stations, entrance areas, etc. Posted signs are explicit so there should be no question. If in doubt, ask. Generally dogs and other pets are not allowed on the Backbone Trail. Bicycles are allowed on fireroads but not on trails. Signs will be placed where these rules change. Some trails exclude horses. This book gives some information on the status of equestrian and bicycle use of the Backbone Trail system. By State law designated Wilderness areas exclude all wheeled vehicles. The trail goes through some of these areas.

Smoking and other fires are not allowed in the back country. You may camp only in designated campgrounds and then by permit.

Temporary closures of parts of the trail can occur at any time. Fire in the mountains, or a high, dry wind from the northeast will be cause for closure. High temperatures or low humidity or even flood conditions will close the area. A daily updated recorded status of the State Parks may be obtained by dialing (213) 454-2372. When we begin to use the Backbone Trail extensively I would expect its inclusion in the fire hazard status report.

Do not remove flowers, rocks, or any natural item. Do not litter or deface the environment.

Each trail segment write-up has basic information. Trailhead maps and the charts can be used to get to the starting point. The trip narrative describes the general idea of the hike or ride with specific attention to the detail of forks in the trail, landmarks, and other items of interest.

Other information may be included in the trip write-up. I have avoided making reference to archaeological sites because their protection is important. My main intent, however, emphasizes the information needed to get on the trail and to your destination.

The book is written as if one were going east to west. These trails can be walked both ways. I have no reason for selecting east to west, but I know someone will ask. Maybe it is because most hikes start in the morning and we don't look into the sun. In any event the maps and distance charts function both directions.

Maps

Each trail section in this book has a map. The map can be used in conjunction with the write-up to aid clarification. To get the most from the experience one might want maps that give more information than the bare essentials. I recommend the 7.5 minute topographic maps published by the U.S. Geological Survey, and topo maps published by Tom Harrison.

The 7.5 minute topos have a scale of 1 inch = 2000 feet, the contour interval of 25 feet makes it possible to estimate elevation gains and losses with reasonable accuracy. The maps do not have an explanation of the symbols used. Tom Harrison's maps are to the same scale and contour interval. He has updated the trail information and explains the symbols used.

Street maps of the local towns are a help in locating trail-heads. The Thomas Guide of Los Angeles and Ventura counties is a convenient reference.

Maps are available from a number of sources. Santa Monica Mountains National Recreation Area, 30401 Agoura Road, Suite 100, Agoura Hills, CA 91301; and most of the backpacking stores in southern California carry them. The Santa Monica Mountains Conservancy has maps of the Santa Monica Mountains as well as the parks under their management. Each State Park has published maps.

If all you planned was a trip on the Backbone Trail this book should be adequate. The next refinement could be the addition of topo maps of the area of your trip. Thirteen topo maps in the 7.5 minute and one 5 x 10 minute series cover the Santa Monica Mountains. The following chart shows the maps. You would not need all of them for the Backbone Trail.

The symbols and key used for maps in this book are on the maps themselves. I've tried to be consistent.

	Camarillo	Newbury Park	Thousand Oaks	Calabasas	Canoga Park	VanNuys	Burbank
Point Mugu		Triunfo Pass	Point Dume	Malibu Beach	Topanga	Beverly Hills	Hollywood

48

Trailheads

ALONG THE BACKBONE TRAIL

(Numbers correspond with those on the map: pages 54 through 58

1   WILL ROGERS STATE HISTORIC PARK
       14253 Sunset Boulevard
       Pacific Palisades, CA 90272
       213/454-8212

       Drive 3.8 miles on Sunset Blvd from Pacific Coast Hwy
       or 4.5 miles from San Diego Fwy. At the Park sign turn
       onto the Park road.
       Parking lot.   Fee.
       Restroom, picnic area, information.

2   TRIPPET RANCH, TOPANGA STATE PARK
       20825 Entrada Road
       Topanga, CA 90290
       213/455-2465

       Drive one-half mile north of the Post Office in Topanga
       on Hwy 27. Turn east on Entrada Road; follow it 1.1
       miles turning left at every opportunity.
       Parking lot.   Fee.
       Restroom, picnic area, pay phone, information.

3   DEAD HORSE TRAILHEAD
       Entrada Road
       Topanga

       Drive one-half mile north of the Post Office in Topanga
       on Hwy 27. Turn east on Entrada Road and almost
       immediately turn left into the parking lot.
       Free parking.
       Restroom.

4   RED ROCK TRAILHEAD

Drive 2 miles north of Hwy 27 on Old Topanga Canyon
Road. Turn west and walk (or drive) to the Red Rock
parking lot.
Restroom, pay phone, picnic area, 4-car parking.

5   STUNT ROAD/SADDLE PEAK ROAD/SCHUEREN ROAD
        JUNCTION.

Drive any of these roads to the intersection with the
others. Park off the road on the north side.
No facilities.
(The trail east has not been built. The trail west is
under construction.)

6   SADDLE CREEK TRAILHEAD

Drive 2.9 miles on Stunt Road from Mulholland Highway.
Park off the left side of the road. (This trailhead is one-
half mile from the Backbone Trail but has been the access
since 1987, during the building of the trail segment. The
east end of the Saddle Peak segment is under construction
(1990) and upon completion, trailhead #6 will be a more
convenient parking area.)
Limited parking
No facilities.

7   DARK CANYON TRAILHEAD

Drive 1.1 mile on Piuma Road from Las Virgenes Road
(Malibu Canyon Road) to the first U-turn on the right.
Park nearby, off the road.
Limited parking.
No facilities.

8   PIUMA TRAILHEAD

Drive 5.2 miles from the Ventura Freeway or 4.5 miles
from the Pacific Coast Highway on Las Virgenes Road
(Malibu Canyon Road) to a parking lot on the west, just
south of the only bridge crossing Malibu Creek.
Free parking.
Restroom.

9   TAPIA PARK TRAILHEAD

Drive 5 miles from the Ventura Freeway or 4.7 miles from
the Pacific Coast Highway on Las Virgenes Road (Malibu
Canyon Road) to a parking lot on the west, north of the
only bridge crossing Malibu Creek.
Free parking (1990)
Restroom.
Picnic area.

10   MALIBU CREEK STATE PARK

Drive 3.6 miles from the Ventura Freeway or 6.1 miles
from the Pacific Coast Highway on Las Virgenes Road
(Malibu Canyon Road) to the entrance on the west. A fee
is charged for parking.
Restrooms.
Camping.

11   CORRAL CANYON ROAD TRAILHEAD

Drive about 2.3 miles west of Malibu Canyon Road on
Pacific Coast Highway and turn right on Corral Canyon
Road. Drive 5.5 miles uphill on this winding road to and
beyond the end of the pavement. Park.
Large parking lot.
No facilities.

12   LATIGO CANYON ROAD TRAILHEAD

From the Ventura Freeway go south on Kanan Dume Road
6.7 miles to Latigo Canyon Road. Drive 3 miles from
Kanan Dume Road on Latigo Canyon Road. Park in an
unpaved lot on the east side of the road.
No facilities.

13   KANAN DUME ROAD TRAILHEAD

From the Ventura Freeway go south 7.8 miles on Kanan
Road to a parking lot on the west side of the road, north
of the tunnel. (About 1.8 miles south of Mulholland
Highway.)
Large parking lot.
No facilities.

14   UPPER TRANCAS CANYON TRAILHEAD

From Kanan Road (County Route N9) go west on
Mulholland Highway .9 mile to the junction with Encinal
Canyon Road (the left fork). Continue about 2.5 miles on
Encinal Canyon Road to a dirt road on the left. Park
nearby, off the road. Do not park on the fireroad or
block the gate.
No facilities.
(Backbone Trail has not been built into Trancas.)
The south end of the 1/2 mile long Clarke Ranch road
begins across Encinal Canyon Road.

15

One or more trailheads will likely be established between
Trancas and Circle X Ranch, but land for the Backbone
Trail between these points has not been acquired (1990).

16   CIRCLE X RANCH, EAST GATE TRAILHEAD

On the west end it is called Yerba Buena Road; at the
east end it is Little Sycamore Canyon Road. The Circle

X Ranch is half way from either end of this eleven miles
of mountainous road. The East Gate Trailhead is one mile
east of Circle X Headquarters.
Large parking lot.
Nearest facilities (restroom, picnic area, information) at
Circle X.

17   SYCAMORE CANYON TRAILHEAD

Drive west of Malibu Canyon Road on the Pacific Coast
Highway 19.1 miles to Sycamore Canyon. Park in area
north of the highway.

18   RAY MILLER TRAILHEAD (La Jolla Canyon)

Drive west of Malibu Canyon Road on the Pacific Coast
Highway 20.7 miles to the Thornhill Broome Beach sign.
Turn right into La Jolla Canyon and go to the Ray Miller
Trailhead. Parking lot, rest rooms. Equestrians take a
right fork and park at the staging area. Gate to the
equestrian area is usually locked — check with Point Mugu
State Park ranger in advance if you plan to ride horses.

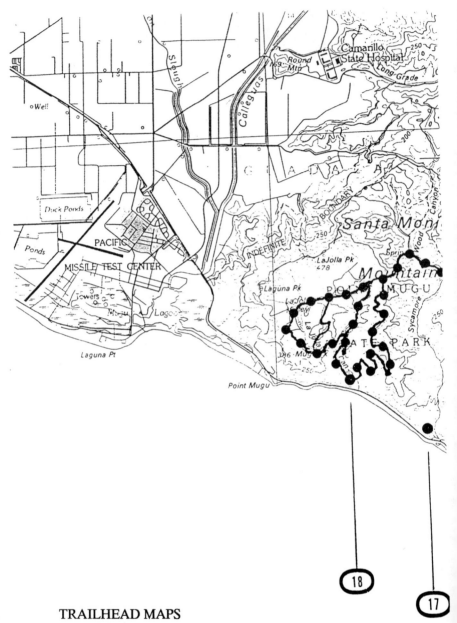

TRAILHEAD MAPS

Five pages of the Backbone Trail show the location of major trailheads. The numbers on the maps correspond with the descriptive instructions on pages 49 through 53.

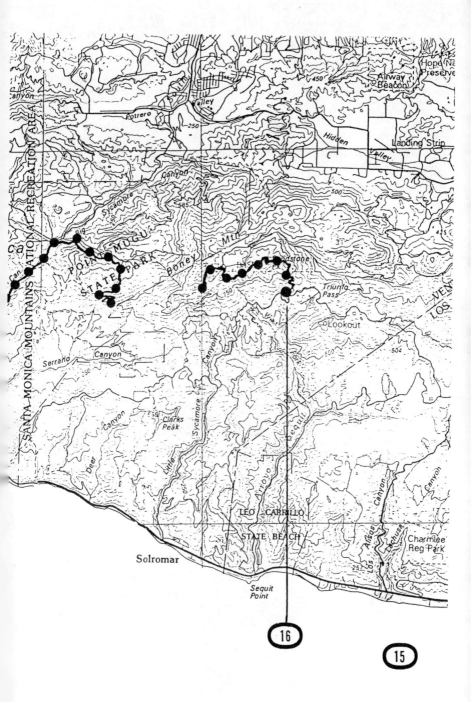

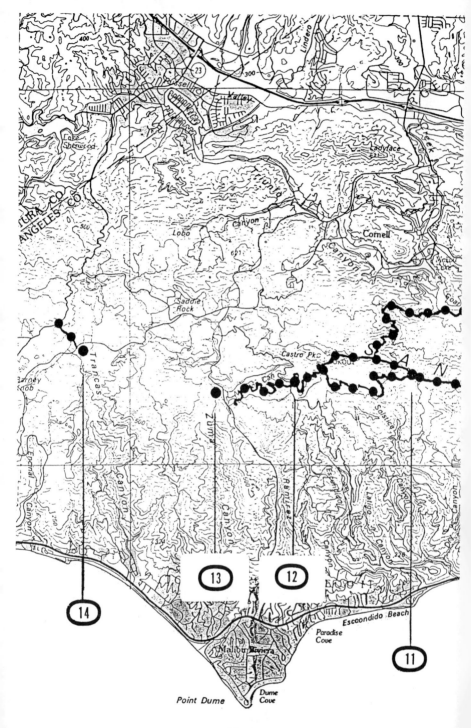

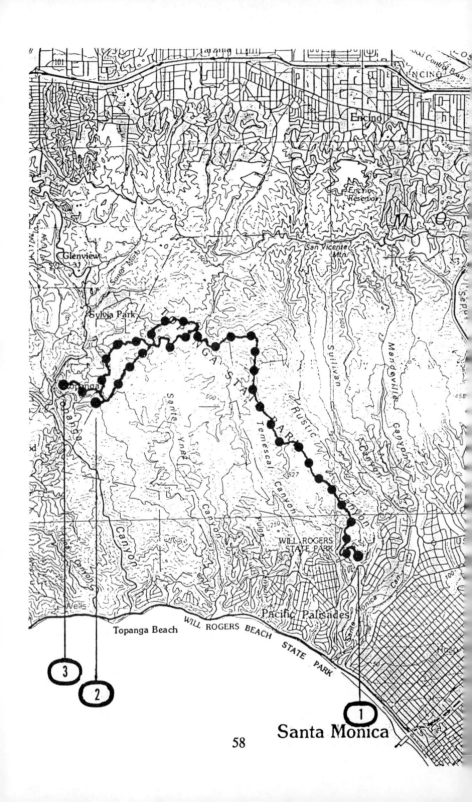

Encino

NCINO

Encino
Reservoir

San Vicente
Mtn

Glenview

Sylvia Park

TOPANGA STATE PARK

Topanga

Santa Ynez Canyon

Temescal Canyon

Rustic Canyon

Sullivan Canyon

Mandeville Canyon

Canyon

WILL ROGERS
STATE PARK

Wells

Pacific Palisades

Topanga Beach

WILL ROGERS BEACH
STATE PARK

Santa Monica Canyon

③

②

①

Santa Monica

58

WILL ROGERS STATE HISTORIC PARK
TO TRIPPET RANCH

Most of us are pleasantly surprised to get off the bus at the Evans Road stop on Sunset Boulevard and step onto the trail going up the slope to Will Rogers State Historic Park. Officially, the beginning of the Backbone Trail is at the park itself, but for the purists among us, starting on Sunset Boulevard in Pacific Palisades gives a romantic slant to the beginning of a memorable walk.

Just because you are in the middle of a sprawling metropolis and may have encountered traffic gridlock getting here, don't overlook the remoteness one feels once on this section of trail. Deer hide out in the brush on the hillside above Sunset Boulevard. They must be inured to street noises because the back country has lots of space and much more solitude. Possibly the deer have an affinity for civilization — as we do — knowing that relief is but a few miles up the trail. Look for them — you may only hear a crashing through the brush, but again you might get lucky with a flashing glimpse of a bounding animal. This short trail crests out near the Polo Field.

Will Rogers, a one-time cowboy from Oklahoma, bought a 348 acre ranch off Sunset Boulevard in 1922. Now a State Park, this land is a fitting terminus for the eastern end of the Backbone Trail. Will built riding and hiking trails about the ranch and we will take one of them as a start of the 65-mile trek of the Backbone Trail.

The Will Rogers State Historic Park is at 14253 Sunset Blvd. in Pacific Palisades. It's a 3.8-mile drive from the Pacific Coast Highway or 4.5 miles from the San Diego Freeway. If you come by RTD bus get off at Evans Road and take the trail uphill to the Polo Field. If you drive, come in on the State Park road. A fee is charged for parking.

You won't have much time to look around if your plan is to walk the nine miles to the Musch Ranch overnight campground or the ten miles to Trippet Ranch, but a tour of the ranch house will take you back to life during the 1920s. Stop at the Visitor Center to be assigned a tour group or pick up an audio cassette for a self-guided tour. Will's ranch house is a museum with everything original. A statue of a calf was made by sculptor Edward Boren so that Will could practice roping in the house without lassoing any guest within range. The 18-room house, with 11 baths and 7 fire-places sits to the side of a large lawn surrounded by a stable, corral, riding rings, and picnic tables. A 12-minute movie on Will's life is shown at the Visitor Center.

James P. Kenney

Home of Will Rogers

Mile 0.0 Begin the hike by taking a trail from the west side of the tennis courts. Several trails can be used to get started. The one described here follows the west fireroad, making a sweep around Inspiration Point. Not too steep and on a well maintained tread, this trail gives you a chance to warm up before reaching the steep part ahead. Uphill from the start, the trail overlooks Rivas Canyon, then passes close to Inspiration Point. A sign on the left at a trail junction indicates the route, beginning a steady uphill climb on Rogers Ridge.

Rogers Ridge runs north and south, dividing Rivas Canyon on the west and Rustic Canyon the east. The ridge comes down from the Santa Monica Mountains ending at Will Rogers State Historic Park. The Backbone Trail works its way up the ridge, past Chicken Ridge — a narrow knife edge now comfortably widened by the construction of a bridge-like causeway. Many views of the ocean will be seen along the trail but take time now to stop and look out on the ocean and Santa Monica Bay. Palos Verdes Peninsula and Santa Catalina Island sit on the horizon. Little shade and a southern exposure make this a hot trail in summer.

Chicken Ridge Bridge

The trail eases up comfortably on top of the ridge with some downhill and uphill as you go from one little peak to another. At a saddle along the ridge a side trail breaks sharply to the right and goes 700 feet down the slope into Rustic Canyon. At one time a plan to build an overnight campground in the canyon was discussed so that through-hikers and equestrians would have a place to stay

61

near Will Rogers SHP. At this same point the Backbone Trail angles left and contours along the west facing slope of the ridge. An alternate and seldom used trail stays on the ridge as the main trail forks left. This old "Rogers Ridge Trail" is usually overgrown and narrow but does offer a commanding view of the impressive Rustic Canyon. The two trails rejoin in about a mile. At the head of Rivas Canyon, the trail makes a sharp left turn and angles northwest. A multi-trunked oak tree here is the best shade in sight. Soon after, you will find yourself walking north on a ridge with Temescal Canyon on the left. An hour later, the trail makes a sweeping turn left, temporarily downhill, and heads for an intersection with Temescal Fireroad. The fireroad is on the north-south ridge between Temescal Canyon and Santa Ynez Canyon.

James P. Kenney

The Tree

At a semi-level stretch of the trail, the Bay Tree Trail joins and heads down to the right on the north facing slope into a west fork of Rustic Canyon. The trail is steep, losing 800 feet in not much over a mile. At the west fork streambed the Bay Tree Trail continues another half mile reaching the Rustic Canyon Trail.

When you reach Temescal fireroad you will have walked six and a third miles. Signs at this intersection read:

to the north	Eagle Junction 1.8 miles
	Ranger Station 4. miles
to the south	Conference Grounds 4.4 miles
to the east	Will Rogers 6.0 miles

(The Conference Grounds 4.4 miles south is a church run facility in Temescal Canyon.)

Go through the gap to a lunch spot in Cathedral Rock

Turn right and in ten minutes you will come to "The Hub," a 4-way intersection of fireroads, and the first restroom since Will Rogers SHP. Before reaching the "Hub," notice "Cathedral Rock" to the east of the Backbone Trail. Cathedral Rock is reached by a

63

short but steep and rocky, trail that goes through a gap into a protected enclosure. Eat lunch here.

At the Hub, the fireroad straight ahead goes 2 miles ending at Mulholland Drive. The next road left, at the Hub, is the upper road of Eagle Spring Loop and will take you high on the ridge overlooking Garapito Canyon and near Eagle Rock. The third road, and left of the upper road, is the lower part of Eagle Spring Loop and will take you downhill past Eagle Spring. Both the upper and lower roads meet at Eagle Junction. Both are considered Backbone Trail routes.

The Outhouse at the Hub

If you elect to walk the upper road, notice the pattern of the diabase rock underfoot as you reach the highest point. Diabase is volcanic rock that intruded through cracks in the earth's surface about 12-to 15-million years ago. Because the molten rock cooled slowly underground, it formed in large crystal-like shapes having a hard center. As the one-to two-foot diameter crystals erode out of the soil, pressure is released and the outer surface exfoliates. We use the term "Onion rock" to describe it. The roadcut after passing

Eagle Rock has good examples. Before reaching Eagle Rock, Garapito Trail starts on the right and drops about 1,000 feet to Garapito Creek, then climbs up to Fireroad 30 — a total distance of 3¼ miles. Just beyond Garapito Trail, Penny Road on the right drops down to the west and leaves the Park. By following Penny Road, then Callon Road, and then Cheney Drive, one could reach Highway #27 (Topanga Canyon Boulevard) about 2 miles north of the town of Topanga. As you continue on the upper loop trail a short path goes to the top of Eagle Rock. Stay on the main fireroad passing Eagle Rock then downhill to Eagle Junction.

Eagle Rock

Eagle Rock is sandstone. The volcanic diabase (Onion rock) intruded a few hundred yards southwest. A fault zone between the two different rock formations can be located. Only geologists would be interested. Of general interest, however, are the "Onion rocks" in the roadcut on the left going downhill after leaving Eagle Rock. These brownish-rust colored volcanic diabase rocks are weathering. Internal pressure release causes this ususual rock structure.

If you decide to take the lower route from the Hub you will pass Eagle Spring. The spring quietly originates as seepage out of the sandstone rock in upper Santa Ynez Canyon. A small dam retains enough water for wild animal needs. Wooden tanks near the road once were filled from a pipe, but these have collapsed and the wood hauled away. Continue west to Eagle Junction.

At Eagle Junction the Backbone Trail again takes two routes. The right trail (Musch Ranch Trail) drops down to a campground at Musch Ranch. Overnight camping, showers, restrooms, and water are available.

The campground at Musch Ranch. Horse corrals are on the left; camping on the right under eucalyptus trees.

The Musch Ranch Trail is the site of fires in the chaparral over a long period of time. The Topanga Canyon fires of 1948, 1961, and 1977 are of recent history as is the prescribed burn of 1984. All of these fires burned over what is now Musch Ranch Trail. Of interest to users of the trail is that frequent burning has set back the chaparral, opening up opportunities for wild flower displays. The left trail stays on a ridge following the fireroad, turning right at the Latitude to Trippet Ranch. The distance between Eagle Junction and Trippet by way of Musch Ranch is 2.2 miles. The distance by fireroad is 1.5 miles.

Trippet Ranch is headquarters for Topanga State Park. The address is 20825 Entrada Road, Topanga, CA 90290. The phone number is presently (213) 455-2465. A pay telephone, parking lot (fee), picnic ground, rest rooms, and a self-guided nature trail are available. A ranger lives at the house south of the parking lot. Another ranger lives at Musch Ranch.

Comments on side trails along this segment:

Mile 0.0 An alternate route, although not the Backbone Trail, leaves from the east end of the Polo Field at Will Rogers State Historic Park and winds down to the stream at the bottom of Rustic Canyon. Going upstream, the trail disappears in places, but if you like boulder hopping and bushwhacking, give it a try on a hot day because the shade helps. A concrete dam built about 1900 by the Santa Monica Land and Water Company has long since filled with rock, sand, and gravel. The trail skirts to the left.

When the motion picture industry was in its infancy, many Westerns were made in lower Rustic Canyon. The canyon was untouched and natural, so it made a real Wild West setting. Later in the 1920s the canyon became a weekend retreat and hikers and equestrians pioneered trails into the upper canyon. During the 1930s Anatol Josepho built a home that was opened to use by servicemen during World War II. In 1941 he bought 100 acres upstream and gave it to the Boy Scouts of America. Camp Josepho thrives today and has been a place for an outdoor experience for thousands of Boy Scouts.

In 1933 a 50 acre parcel of fenced area built up. It included a water tank, diesel fuel tank, power station, and living areas. the story persists that this was a pro-Nazi community to be used as a refuge in case of war with Germany. The property now belongs to Los Angeles and is part of the Park.

Farther upstream a steep trail leads up the slope to the west and joins the Backbone Trail on top. At one time plans were to build an overnight camp down in the canyon. If the vision of groups of hikers and equestrians making through-trips on the Backbone Trail is to become reality, overnight campgrounds are needed.

67

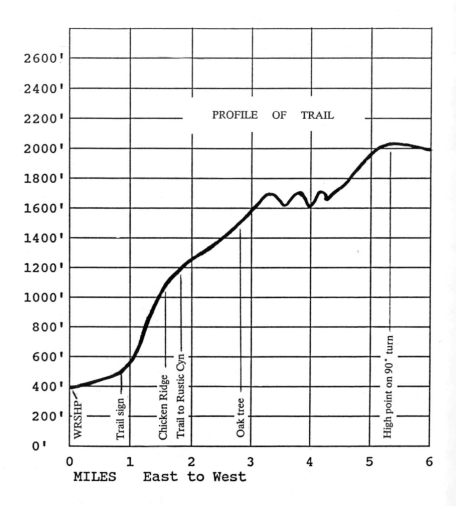

68

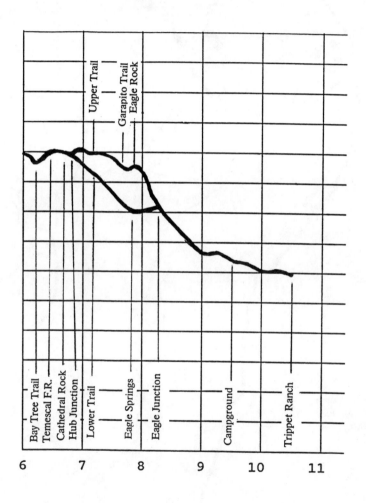

69

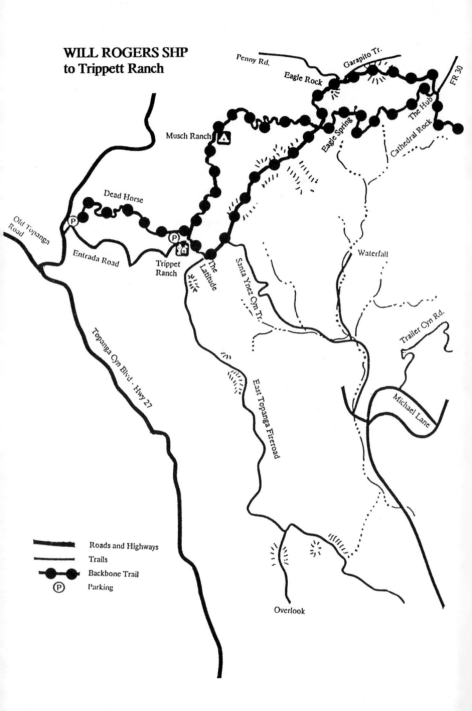

WILL ROGERS SHP
to Trippett Ranch

Penny Rd.

Garapito Tr.

Eagle Rock

FR 30

The Hub

Musch Ranch

Eagle Spring

Cathedral Rock

Dead Horse

Waterfall

Old Topanga Road

Entrada Road

Trippet Ranch

The Latitude

Santa Ynez Cyn Tr.

Trailer Cyn Rd.

Michael Lane

Topanga Cyn Blvd - Hwy 27

East Topanga Fireroad

Overlook

━━━ Roads and Highways
─── Trails
●━● Backbone Trail
Ⓟ Parking

70

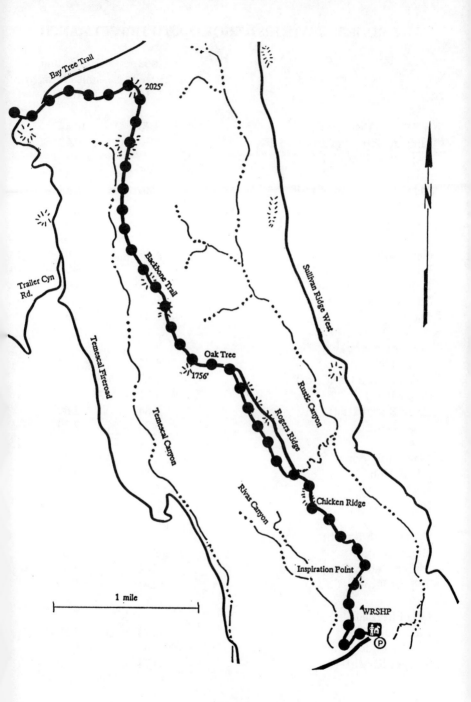

Bay Tree Trail

2025'

Trailer Cyn Rd.

Temescal Fireroad

Backbone Trail

Temescal Canyon

Oak Tree

1756'

Rogers Ridge

Sullivan Ridge West

Rustic Canyon

Rivas Canyon

Chicken Ridge

Inspiration Point

WRSHP

N

1 mile

71

WILL ROGERS STATE HISTORIC PARK TO TRIPPET RANCH

	Westbound miles from WRSHP	Eastbound miles from TRIPPET
WRSHP (Visitor's Center)	0.00	10.44
Junction with Inspiration Pt. FR via West Fireroad	0.94	9.50
Bridge at Chicken Ridge	1.61	8.83
Saddle at junction of trail to Rustic Cyn	1.86	8.58
Oak Tree via Rivas Tr.	2.97	7.47
Trail to Peak 1756	3.37	7.07
High point of 90° turn	5.39	5.05
Junction with Bay Tree Tr.	6.24	4.20
Temescal FR junction	6.35	4.09
Cathedral Rock (trail)	6.72	3.72
The Hub	6.85	3.59
(Via north loop)		
The Hub	6.85	3.59
Junction with Garapito Tr.	7.69	2.75
Penny Road	7.71	2.73
Eagle Rock (Trail)	7.84	2.60
Eagle Junction	8.24	2.20
(Via south loop)		
The Hub	6.85	3.59
Eagle Springs	7.86	2.60
Eagle Junction	8.22	2.20
(Via Musch Ranch)		
Eagle Junction	8.24	2.20
Musch Ranch Campground	9.44	1.00
Trippet Ranch	10.44	0.00
(Via Fireroad)		
Eagle Junction	8.24	1.50
The Latitude	9.44	0.30
Trippet Ranch	9.74	0.00

DEAD HORSE TRAIL SEGMENT
TRIPPET RANCH TO DEAD HORSE TRAILHEAD

In the 1890s Mr. Robinson homesteaded 80 acres on the west boundary of the San Vicente y Santa Monica Rancho (a Mexican land grant). Oscar Trippet bought the homestead in 1917 and used the property as a weekend retreat. The buildings in use today were built in the late 1930s and early '40s. Topanga State Park opened for public use on 1 July 1973 with Trippet Ranch as headquarters and main entrance.

James P. Kenney

The wooden bridge along Dead Horse Trail

The Dead Horse Trail is about 1¼ miles long. The east end is at Trippet Ranch; the west end at the Dead Horse trailhead. The trail was built in the late 1970s by a Sierra Club volunteer team. During construction the crew suggested different names for the trail until one day as the trail neared completion, the crew arrived at the trailhead to find that overnight someone had buried a small horse in the trail. "Dead Horse Trail" has been the name since.

James P. Kenney

Dead Horse Trail through the oak woodland

From the picnic area at Trippet, walk past a bulletin board and head north across the small dam. Turn left and hike west on the trail at the edge of the oak woodland. The trail is almost level until it leaves the oaks and enters a chapparal forest. Then you start a downhill grade that is usually gentle with two or three short, steep sections. Two-thirds of the way to the trailhead you drop down to a riparian woodland of sycamore and bay trees. The trail crosses a stream on a wooden bridge installed in 1986. The bridge was brought in without damaging the environment — a highly responsible bit of engineering. Take time to savor the shade in the creek canyon because a lot of the Backbone Trail is in the sun, and shade is rare.

At the bridge you might risk poison oak and climb down to the streambed. The original trail — before the bridge was built — goes to the stream. Vegetation has grown so don't expect a clear path. A small waterfall, pools of water, sweet cicely, geranium, grape, and four species of fern grow along the banks.

The trail comes closer to civilization as it approaches the parking lot at the Dead Horse Trailhead.

Because this trail starts near a pond, goes along the edge of a meadow, in and out of coast live oaks, and then through pure chaparral before dropping down to a riparian woodland by a stream, you will see a wide variety of plant communities. This gives the botanist in you an excellent chance to see the ever-changing biotic variation along the trail.

Most of the trail is on sandstone until the last stretch which is on basalt, a fine-grained volcanic rock. The final 100 feet to the parking lot, is steeper, and the solid basalt is covered with imported gravel making the tread a little unsteady.

The Dead Horse trailhead is one-half mile north of the Topanga Post Office on Topanga Canyon Blvd. Turn east on Entrada Road, go 100 yards and turn left into the parking lot. We must take care driving into the parking lot coming uphill on Entrada. The turn into the lot is left on a blind curve.

Restrooms are available. The lot is closed and locked at night. Parking is free. This may change.

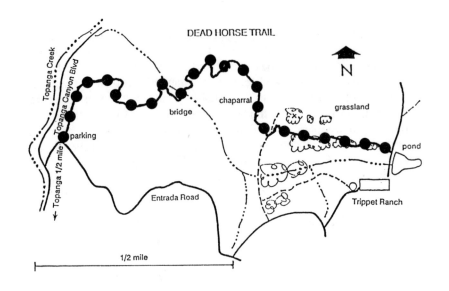

DEAD HORSE TRAIL

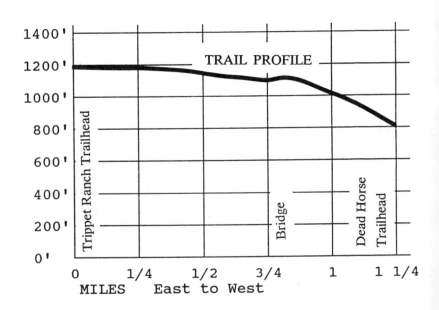

TRAIL PROFILE

MILES   East to West

DEAD HORSE TRAILHEAD
TO SADDLE PEAK TRAILHEAD

This segment of the Backbone Trail will be built later. I estimate the segment will be 6 miles long — and that will depend upon the final alignment. The trail corridor was procured in the early 1980s and since then some alignment decisions have been made. The big decision and the challenge, is the route in upper Hondo Canyon. Without a doubt this section of trail will offer spectacular scenery.

The likely alignment will be from Dead Horse Trailhead to Greenleaf Canyon Road, then west over Henry Ridge to Topanga Meadows. There, an existing trail heads west along a side stream. At some point, the trail will be rerouted to cross over the stream and up a sloping meadow on the north to pick up an existing trail,

A preliminary trail through Topanga Meadows
(Not open for Backbone travel)

77

making a loop into a beautiful oak woodland. Climbing again, the proposed trail will make another switchback to gain the ridge overlooking Hondo Canyon. Going west, the trail will cross the crest into Hondo Canyon. A flagged alignment contours along the north facing slope of the canyon wall reaching an existing trail that follows a short distance up Hondo Canyon. From the end of that trail one of the major trail building projects for the Backbone Trail will begin — in Upper Hondo Canyon. (Not everyone knows the meaning of the following terms: "Switchback," on a trail, is a sudden reversal of direction for the purpose of maintaining a gentle walking slope [less than 10°] while climbing a steep hill. "Flag": On the Backbone Trail a plastic strip is tied to a branch by the trail designer. Later, maybe years, a trail building crew will dig the tread so that the flag will be at eye level for someone 5'10".)

Alternate (temporary) route through Red Rock Canyon.

Until the trail between the Dead Horse Trail and the Saddle Peak Trail is built we can use an alternate existing route through Red Rock Canyon.

Red Rock Canyon Trail

78

From the Dead Horse Trailhead go south 1/2 mile on Topanga Canyon Boulevard turning right on Old Topanga Road. Drive 2 miles to Red Rock Road and turn left. Find a place to park off the road or drive 3/4 mile to a 4-car parking area near a locked gate. Purists may want to walk the 3¼ miles to Red Rock. If so, leave Dead Horse from the northeast corner of the parking lot and go down to Topanga Canyon Boulevard on an old trail. Cross the highway at Greenleaf Canyon and if you are really adventurous and have no fear of poison oak, you could continue west on Greenleaf one hundred feet. Get off the road to the left and bushwhack up the ridge, gaining 300 feet of altitude in about 1/2 mile. At the crest (Henry Ridge), continue west on an overgrown steep trail dropping down along the base of a massive cliff of basaltic rock. The trail reaches Old Topanga Road at a point 1/2 mile north of its junction with Topanga Canyon Boulevard. Or you may prefer to walk along the road to Red Rock. The last time, I went by car. (Needed to check the mileage for this book).

After going around the gate and past an occupied house, head west up Red Rock Road. Somewhat of an oddity, but standing under the trees is a phone booth. It's a couple hundred feet beyond the gate and it works. Camp Slauson, a Boy Scout weekend camping area, occupied the canyon before the Santa Monica Mountains Conservancy bought the property. Boys phone home easier than they write.

A 600 foot gain during a 45-minute walk puts you on a ridge and at an intersection with the road coming down from Calabasas Peak. Turn left and in 15 minutes reach Stunt Road.

Cross the road and at the far end of the parking lot head down the trail to Cold Creek. You may notice some bees flying to the nearby flowers. About 90 hives are stacked on a flat area left of the trail. After crossing the stream the trail turns right and follows along the edge of the bank. After a delightful 1/2 mile under a canopy of oak, sycamore and a maple tree, a trail intersects on the left. At this point look for some Indian mortars in a large sandstone boulder. Acorns were processed here, probably by the Indians that once lived near where the Stunt Ranch now stands.

A bedrock mortar used for acorn grinding.

Keep to the left and go uphill in a southerly direction reaching Stunt Road after twenty minutes of hiking. About 200 yards west of the parking lot to the Stunt High Trail, cross the road. This trail gains about 350 feet as it wanders one mile in a southerly direction. The Stunt High Trail ends at Stunt Road 1.1 miles from a parking area on Saddle Peak Road. Limited parking is available at the end of Stunt High Trail.

You may elect to walk or ride 1.1 miles up Stunt Road to the parking area for the eastern end of the Saddle Peak segment of the Backbone Trail. (This parking area will also be at the western terminal of the Hondo Canyon segment — when the segment is built.)

Another option is available at this point. By crossing Stunt Road and going 200 yards downhill you will find a trail on the left. This trail leads to the Backbone Trail segment going west toward Tapia.

Facilities enroute:

Restrooms and water at Dead Horse Trailhead.

Post Office at Topanga Canyon Blvd./Old Topanga Road.

Pay telephone at Red Rock.

Outhouse at Stunt Road parking lot.

DEAD HORSE TO SADDLE PEAK TRAIL

	Westbound miles	Eastbound miles
Dead Horse Trailhead	0.00	8.25
Old Topanga Cyn Rd/Red Rock Rd	2.40	5.85
Red Rock parking	3.15	5.10
Calabasas Motorway junction	4.35	3.90
Stunt Road (and parking lot)	5.05	3.20
Bedrock mortar (on lower Cold Cr) Trail junction to Stunt Ranch	5.55	2.70
Stunt Ranch junction to ranch	5.70	2.55
Stunt Ranch parking lot on Stunt Rd	6.20	2.05
Beginning of Stunt High Trail	6.25	2.00
Stunt High (top parking)	7.15	1.10
Saddle Peak Rd/Stunt Rd	8.25	0.00

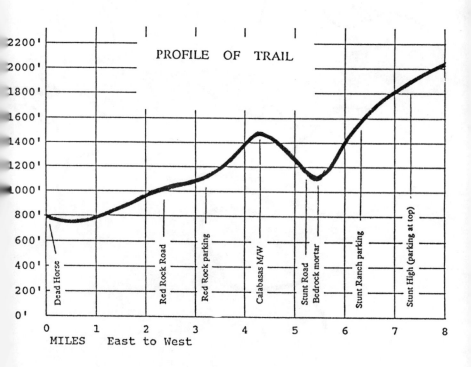

PROFILE OF TRAIL

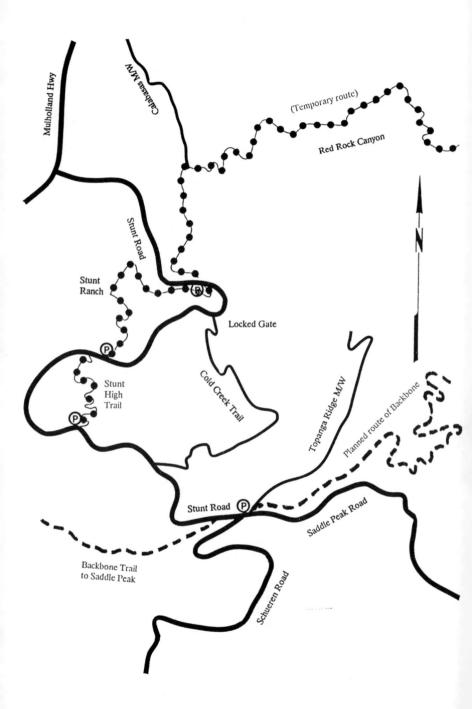

Mulholland Hwy

Calabasas M/W

(Temporary route)

Red Rock Canyon

Stunt Road

Stunt Ranch

Locked Gate

Cold Creek Trail

Stunt High Trail

Topanga Ridge M/W

Planned route of Backbone

Stunt Road

Saddle Peak Road

Backbone Trail to Saddle Peak

Schueren Road

N

82

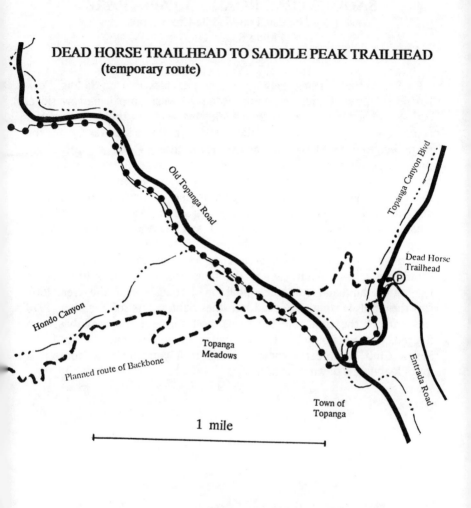

DEAD HORSE TRAILHEAD TO SADDLE PEAK TRAILHEAD
(temporary route)

Old Topanga Road

Topanga Canyon Blvd

Dead Horse Trailhead

Hondo Canyon

Planned route of Backbone

Topanga Meadows

Entrada Road

Town of Topanga

1 mile

Roads & Highways
Trails

Planned route of Backbone Trail
Temporary route of Backbone Trail

SADDLE PEAK ROAD TO TAPIA PARK
(Saddle Peak Trail/Saddle Creek Trail/
Piuma Ridge Trail)

From the parking area at the upper junction of Saddle Peak Road, Schueren Road, and Stunt Road go west onto a narrow ridge. As of publication date of this book this end of the trail has not been completed and a possibility exists of the actual entry to the ridge being a hundred feet or so down Stunt Road on the south side. An old road once came up to the ridge, crossed over and paralleled below the crest on the south side. Because this part of the trail is not yet completed, expect to pick your way around rocks and through buckwheat. Head for a large water tank, enroute passing two houses, both on the right and close to the trail. Please keep in mind that anyone living on an otherwise wild and uninhabited ridge does so out of a preference for peace and tranquility. We should be quiet. After passing the houses aim for the south side of the water tank and continue uphill on a road. Near the crest look for the trail leaving the road on the right. (As of October 1990 this part of the trail and 200 yards west through chaparral has been flagged but not built.) If you can wait a few months until the Sierra Club volunteer crew clears the trail you can save yourself a lot of leaf debris down your neck.

Saddle Peak West from Saddle Peak East

Before leaving Saddle Peak you might want to go to the top and look around. The road turns south and continues left until you are on top. Or are you? A saddle peak is two peaks with a saddle between. We have climbed Saddle Peak East. Saddle Peak West can be reached by walking the road to the fences and communication towers. At 2805 feet it is the highest point in the central or eastern part of the Santa Monica Mountains. Back on the trail, you might prefer to walk west on a rocky sandstone ridge rather than bushwhack. When complete, the trail will be at the north base of the cliff. Walk to the west end of the ridge and climb down to the trail. From here the trail is complete the rest of the way.

Sandstone cliffs dominate the view from high on the trail.

Calabasas Peak is framed by the rocks.

The Picture is taken looking north

Botanists will find this trail exciting. From the top for 150 yards a forest of chaparral pea (*Pickeringia montana*) surrounds you. This 10 foot shrub is not common in the Santa Monica Mountains and this is the finest stand in the eastern half. Look for red-purple flowers in May.

The trail makes an abrupt turn north to wind down among some very large sandstone monoliths. At the first switchback look for silk-tassel bush *(Garrya veatchii)*. On the outside of the next switchback you can see a 15 x 30' patch of ocean spray *(Holodiscus discolor)*, a surprise anywhere. Farther down the trail a sharp eye will find a few of the rare whitethorn *(Ceanothus leucodermis)*.

The Saddle Peak Trail winds through a rocky passageway.

Once starting down the north slope of Saddle Peak we lose altitude constantly from about 2700 feet (2800 feet if we elect to go to the top of Saddle Peak) to 2050 feet, where we reach a somewhat level stretch. Because the State Park trail corridor is narrow and the slope of the hill is steep the trail has 16 switchbacks along this section. As a general rule the Backbone Trail grade is such that 500' of elevation change in one mile of travel is maximum. This part of the trail pushes the limit. Great views of the chaparral covered Cold Creek watershed are below, and Calabasas Peak, 2½ miles north, is constantly in view. Coming back up the trail, one is more likely to at first notice the dominance of Ceanothus oliganthus interspersed with manzanita. Near the top chamise takes over. A fire in 1970 swept this slope burning everything but leaving charred dead trunks of the larger shrubs. These are standing today and much of the new growth (since 1970) sprouted from the root crowns.

At the 2050 foot level we will notice a large eucalyptus tree and a flat area. One hundred yards west — off the trail — a woodland of coast live oaks is a good shady lunch spot.

A volunteer maintenance crew repairing the Saddle Creek segment.

Near the stream crossing in Dark Canyon
Native grapes grow here (upper right in the picture.)
SADDLE CREEK TRAIL

Get back on the trail and almost immediately make a 90° turn west. Avoid the steep side trail used during trail construction. (It continues north and goes to Stunt Road.) Elevation changes are mild for the next half mile or so, as the trail drops in and out of wooded areas, sometimes oaks, sometimes bay trees. On occasion you will walk through delightful corridors flanked by large boulders or past a streambed that would have a small waterfall if we ever get rain. Soon you will notice downhill again and then abruptly come to an overlook of Malibu Creek watershed. Monte Nido is the name of the housing area below and west. Tighten your shoe laces and prepare for an 800 foot drop to the Dark Canyon creek crossing.

Dark Canyon has pools of water even in dry years. A native grape (*Vitis girdiana*) grows at the stream crossing. I have not seen any other native grape vines along the Backbone Trail. White alder trees and bay trees grow along the stream. Flowering ash is found higher on the hillside, then comes chaparral.

Leave the stream for a short climb on the trail to a chaparral ridge before reaching Piuma Road. Two or three cars can park off Piuma Road on the upper side of the turn and a much larger parking area is available several hundred yards down the road. However, for purposes of this hike description, we will cross the road to continue on a 1.5 mile "Piuma Ridge" segment of the Backbone Trail.

Staying high on the hillside to pass well above several houses, the trail contours for about three-fourths mile. Passing through a beautiful grove of bay trees, the trail makes a couple of switchbacks to lose altitude. After crossing a driveway in an oak grove, the trail turns right, then left, to parallel Piuma Road. Being in a streambed subject to flooding, this part of the trail can become undefined at times, or even under water. Normally walk west going under the bridge that crosses Malibu Creek. A picnic area and the parking lot at Tapia Park is the end of this segment of the trail.

The only facilities anywhere along the Saddle Peak/Saddle Creek/Piuma Ridge segment are at Tapia Park. Restrooms, drinking water, picnic tables, and barbeque pits.

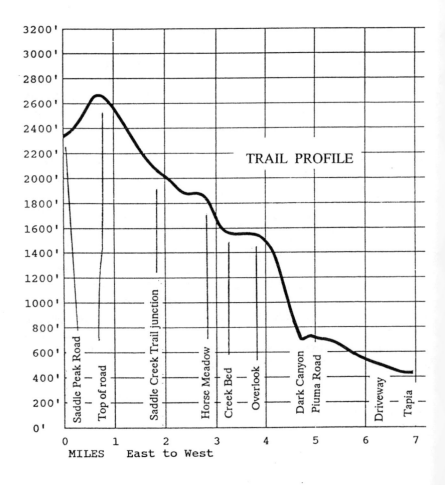

TRAIL PROFILE

Saddle Peak Road
Top of road
Saddle Creek Trail junction
Horse Meadow
Creek Bed
Overlook
Dark Canyon
Piuma Road
Driveway
Tapia

MILES   East to West

90

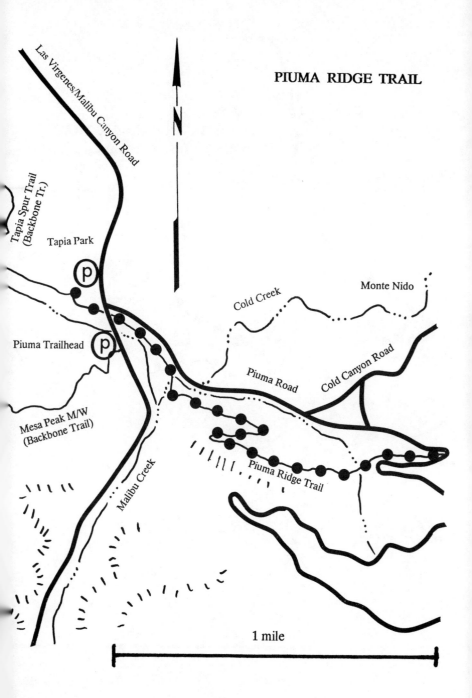

PIUMA RIDGE TRAIL

Las Virgenes/Malibu Canyon Road

Tapia Spur Trail
(Backbone Tr.)

Tapia Park

Cold Creek

Monte Nido

Piuma Trailhead

Cold Canyon Road

Piuma Road

Mesa Peak M/W
(Backbone Trail)

Malibu Creek

Piuma Ridge Trail

1 mile

SADDLE CREEK TRAIL

Cold Creek

Cold Canyon Road

Saddle Creek

1942'

Saddle Creek Trail

Monte Nido

Dark Canyon

Piuma Road

1 mile

92

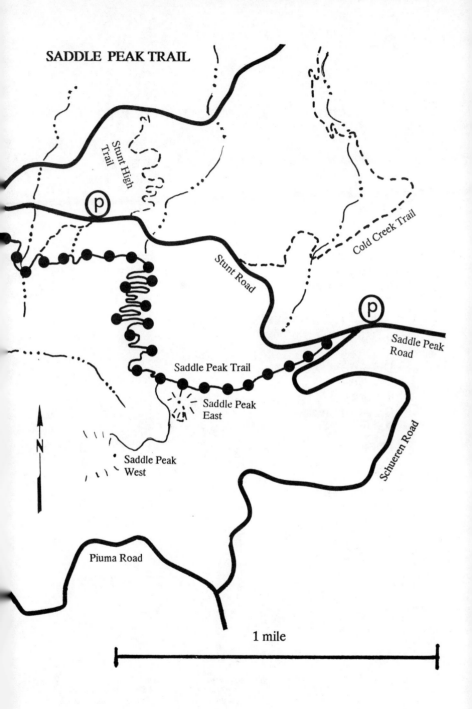

SADDLE PEAK TRAIL

Stunt High Trail

Cold Creek Trail

Stunt Road

Saddle Peak Road

Saddle Peak Trail

Saddle Peak East

Saddle Peak West

Schueren Road

N

Piuma Road

1 mile

93

SADDLE PEAK ROAD TO TAPIA PARK

		Westbound Miles	Eastbound Miles
Saddle Peak Section	Saddle Peak Road	0.00	6.83
	Two houses on ridge	0.26	6.57
	Water tank	0.37	6.46
	Top of road (GTE manhole cover)	0.62	6.21
	Turn onto trail	0.64	6.19
	Large cliffs	0.80	6.03
	Eucalyptus tree	1.72	5.11
	Trail branches west	1.76	5.07
	Saddle Creek Trail junction	1.95	4.88
Saddle Creek Section	Horse Meadow	2.91	3.92
	Creek bed	3.20	3.63
	Overlook	3.99	2.84
	Dark Cyn Creek	4.63	2.20
	Ridge	4.77	2.06
	Piuma Road	4.84	1.99
Piuma Ridge Section	Woodbluff trail	5.11	1.72
	Driveway	6.30	0.53
	Creek Trail intersection	6.36	0.47
	Tapia picnic area	6.75	0.08
	Tapia parking lot	6.83	0.00

TAPIA TO LATIGO CANYON ROAD

From Tapia Park westbound two routes of the Backbone Trail are available: The valley route, and the ridge route. Both meet again in about 9 miles and each presents different aspects of the trail. Both segments are presented here.

TAPIA TO LATIGO CANYON ROAD
via Century Lake and Bulldog M/W

From the Tapia parking lot, go west on a road closed to traffic because of potholes. Keep to the right as the road curves around a wooded hill. Northeast of the Salvation Army entry road, look for a trail to the north. In due time a "Backbone Trail" sign will be placed here.

Built in 1982 by a Sierra Club volunteer team, the trail is an important connecting link with the central part of Malibu Creek State Park. After a 100-yard walk in an oak woodland, the trail abruptly branches left and goes uphill through chaparral. The Dayton Canyon fire of 1982 burned the upper part of the trail soon after it was built. The succession of fire-following plants is in progress along the trail with annual flowering plants being replaced by low growing shrubs to be eventually dominated by chaparral.

A half-mile of uphill to a saddle between two low peaks calls for a rest stop. Behind us to the southeast we can look down to Camp Gonzales, a minimum security facility. Ahead to the north is a view of a somewhat level valley and the joining of Stokes Creek, Las Virgenes Creek, and Malibu Creek. Three hundred yards beyond the saddle brings us to a group campground in an oak woodland. Rest rooms, drinking water, picnic tables and camping are available.

Five minutes down the trail beyond the group campground brings you to a road leading to an RV/trailer campground. Turn left at the road, pass a large Valley oak, cross the Stokes Creek culvert and turn left onto the road leading to the Visitor's Center and the main part of the valley floor. When the trail forks go left to the Visitor's Center or right along the High Road. They rejoin in slightly more than one-half mile. The Visitor's Center is presently open on weekends at noon, and well worth a visit for natural history displays and general information.

If you care to take a side trip after crossing the bridge, turn left on a trail to Rock Pool. Here, back when 20th Century Fox made movies on the location, *Swiss Family Robinson,* and the Tarzan series were filmed. *Planet of the Apes, F-Troop, How Green was my Valley,* and dozens more films used Malibu Creek for outdoor locations. A short walk uphill takes you to a viewpoint overlooking Century Lake. Goat Buttes make a rugged volcanic backdrop for the lake. At the north end of Century Lake where a bridge crosses Malibu Creek, fill your canteen at the drinking fountain. This is the last water on the trail. A 15-minute walk takes you to what was once the *M.A.S.H.* site.

Century Lake. Impounded by a dam built about 1900, the lake is slowly filling with silt.

Rock Pool. After flowing over the dam at Century Lake, Malibu Creek goes behind Goat Buttes then empties into Rock Pool.

Early morning on 9 October 1982 a fire started in Dayton Canyon near the west end of the San Fernando Valley. Twelve hours later homes were burning in Paradise Cove east of Point Dume. On its way to the ocean (the ultimate firebreak) the fire burned 42,000 acres, jumped the Ventura Freeway and all other roads in its path. The fire came through Malibu Creek State Park sparing the creek bed and some of the hillsides, but the *M.A.S.H.* site was directly in its path. The jeep and the ambulance along the trail are about the only reminders that this was the location where *M.A.S.H.* was filmed.

Jeep and ambulance burned at the M.A.S.H. site during the 1982 fire.

A few hundred yards farther along the trail look for the Mendenhall Oak. This landmark, reportedly a meeting place for Joaquin Murietta and his band, was burned and fell to the ground during the fire. Now a branch has grown from the seemingly dead stump, proving that oak trees are indeed survivors.

Bulldog Motorway starts uphill gently on the left, but continues uphill for 3.5 miles gaining 1800 feet before reaching Castro Motorway. Once on the ridge, the next half mile going west is of special interest to botanists. At the junction of Bulldog and Castro look for Santa Susana Tarweed plants, one of which is six feet in diameter and growing. Two other seldom seen plants are plentiful on the south side of the road: Hawkweed growing from cracks in the sandstone and Yerba Santa usually found on flatter soil. A small forest of chaparral pea covers part of the ridge above the road. On the right side of the road look for Wright's buckwheat and silver lotus.

All of the rock along this part of Castro Motorway is of a non-marine sequence named the Sespe Formation. The strata dips northeast on a steep angle, in some places 80°. Sespe was formed during the late Eocene, Oligocene and early Miocene times, 40 to 25 million years ago, when the land was above sea level. Imbedded in sandstone, you can see small rounded boulders polished by rolling in a river bed.

After some more uphill travel, turn left onto Newton Motorway about .6 of a mile beyond Bulldog Motorway. The views both north and south from the Castro Crest part of the trail are phenomenal. Some shade under oaks is available and lunch, or at least a rest stop, is a good decision.

Follow Newton Motorway mostly downhill for another .6 of a mile to a trail on the right. The trail takes you down into Newton Canyon and shade. After crossing the stream, the trail contours out of the canyon, climbing some. One-half mile after leaving the streambed you will coast into the dirt parking lot. You will be glad you put an extra canteen in the car because the last available water was close to 2100 feet of climbing, and more than 7 miles back.

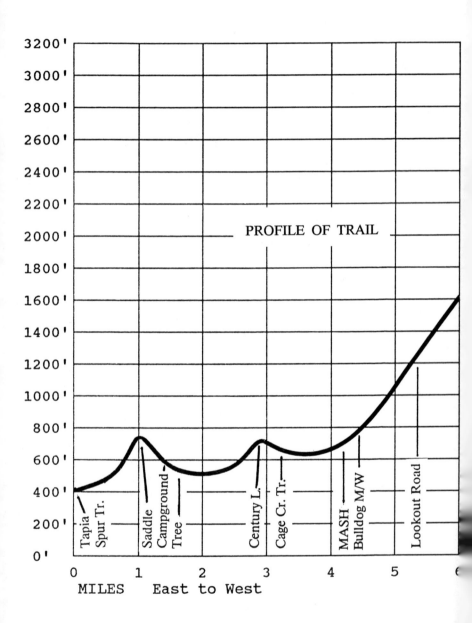

100

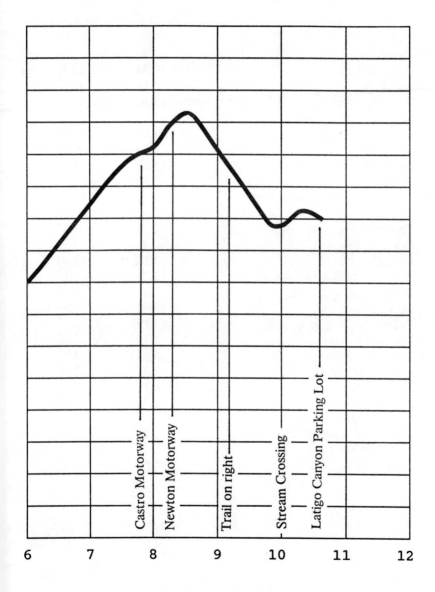

6 7 8 9 10 11 12

101

TAPIA TO LATIGO CANYON ROAD
via Century Lake and Bulldog M/W

	Westbound Miles	Eastbound Miles
Tapia parking lot	0.00	10.50
Tapia Spur Trail	.45	10.05
Trail fork (go left uphill)	.50	10.00
Saddle between Tapia/MCSP	1.05	9.45
Group Campground	1.20	9.30
Road to RV campground	1.50	9.00
Gate opposite MCSP parking lot	1.65	8.85
Fork in trail — left to Visitor's Center, Right to High Road	1.95	8.55
Junction of High Rd & Low Rd	2.55	7.95
Century Lake viewpoint	2.85	7.65
Lookout Trail	2.95	7.55
Cage Creek Trail	3.20	7.30
Bridge & drinking fountain	3.35	7.15
Forest Trail	3.40	7.10
M.A.S.H.	4.00	6.50
Bulldog Motorway	4.25	6.75
Lookout Road	5.35	5.15
Lakeside Lateral	5.60	4.90
Castro Motorway	7.65	2.85
Newton Motorway	8.25	2.25
Trail to Latigo Rd. (turn right onto trail)	9.05	1.45
Streambed crossing in upper Newton Canyon	10.00	.50
Latigo Canyon Road	10.50	0.00

BACKBONE TRAIL/CASTRO
to Latigo Canyon Road

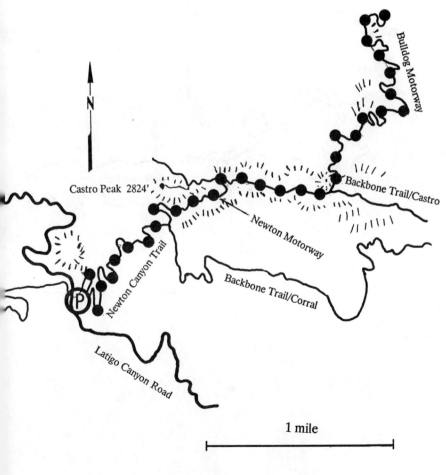

Bulldog Motorway

Castro Peak 2824'

Backbone Trail/Castro

Newton Motorway

Newton Canyon Trail

Backbone Trail/Corral

P

Latigo Canyon Road

N

1 mile

CENTURY LAKE
to Castro M/W

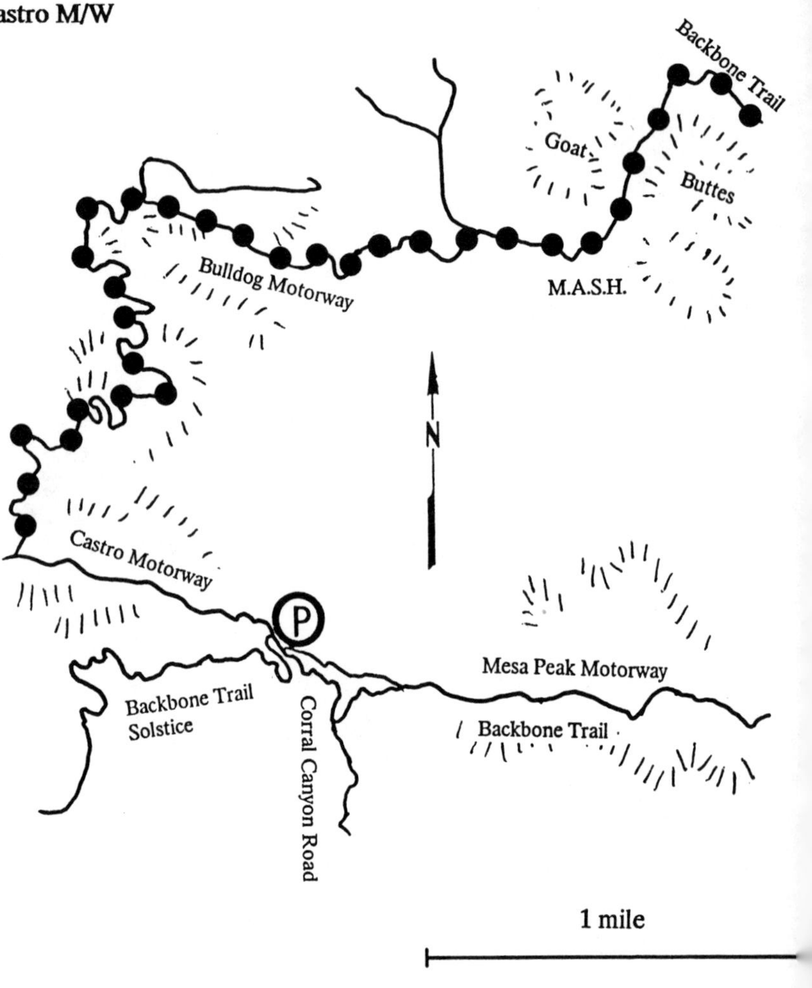

Backbone Trail

Goat

Buttes

Bulldog Motorway

M.A.S.H.

N

Castro Motorway

P

Mesa Peak Motorway

Backbone Trail
Solstice

Corral Canyon Road

Backbone Trail

1 mile

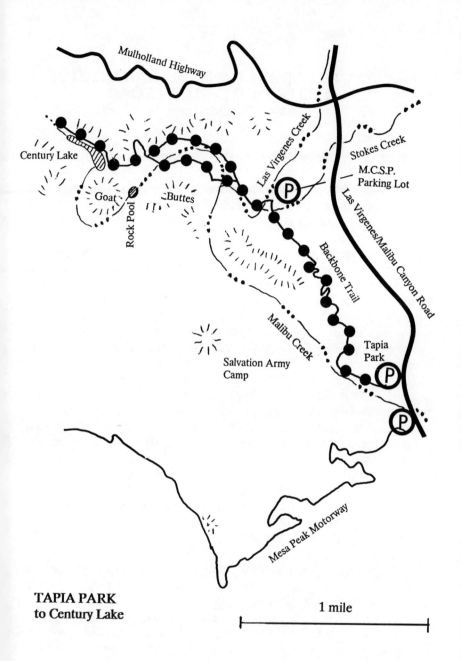

Mulholland Highway

Century Lake

Las Virgenes Creek

Stokes Creek

M.C.S.P.
Parking Lot

℗

Goat

Rock Pool

Buttes

Las Virgenes/Malibu Canyon Road

Backbone Trail

Malibu Creek

Salvation Army
Camp

Tapia
Park

℗

℗

Mesa Peak Motorway

TAPIA PARK
to Century Lake

1 mile

TAPIA TO CORRAL CANYON TRAILHEAD
and TO LATIGO CANYON ROAD
via Mesa Peak Motorway

Park in the Tapia lot or park in the lot south of the bridge at the Piuma Trailhead.

If you park at Tapia, walk south on Malibu Canyon Road, crossing the bridge and turning right into the lot. The trail begins under the pines and makes a left turn beyond the restrooms. In 200 yards make a right turn onto a fireroad.

If you agree that early morning contains the essence of the day, choose this trail for an early start. Uphill most of the way, and on an east facing slope and ridge, you can climb as the sun warms your back. Behind you the Malibu Creek gorge becomes apparent; before the hike is done you will be 1500 feet higher and have many chances to view this magnificent canyon from above.

About a half mile from the trailhead a road branches right and dead-ends at a gate. This is an access road for emergency vehicles and we don't use it. Notice it, though, because some people end up wondering what went wrong — particularly when coming from the west. Stay left, keep climbing, and you begin to pick out the features of the area. Brents Mountain at 1713 feet, with a cross on its peak, is about 1 mile north by west. Beyond, you can see Malibu Creek State Park and Goat Buttes. The ocean is in view to the south. Two and a half miles after starting the hike, look for another trail branch. It is readily visible, but my head is down and I'm plodding at this point so one must stay alert. Keep right at the branch and continue uphill. If you were to find yourself going downhill toward the ocean, stop.

Soon, on the right near a metal water tank, a seldom-used trail will take you to the top of Peak 2049 and a good view. Continuing west, the trail levels out somewhat as you follow the ridge. Look for fossil turritella shells in the roadbed.

About 2½ miles beyond Peak 2049 you will pass some caves in large sandstone outcrops. These pinnacles are a distinctive landmark and make for interesting investigation. During a period of geologic history in the late Eocene, Oligocene, and early Miocene (about 30-40 million years ago), huge amounts of rock and gravel washed down a flood plain and deposited layers of conglomerate on the land. This 3000 foot thick layer, called the Sespe Formation, became tilted during the mountain forming process and here it is almost vertical.

You are about to experience this ridge at close hand. You could stay on the motorway if you like and intercept Corral Road about one-third mile away, but if a short 30° grade is no threat go up a path on the right, through the rocks. Two routes separated by a ten-foot rock ridge parallel each other for the two-hundred-foot distance to the crest. Take either route. It looks steep from below but the footing is solid, and on the other side the trail winds through the rocks. At the gap on top look west to see "Hole in the Rock." North and east of this point on the trail an uncommon low shrub, Wrights' buckwheat (*Eriogonum wrightii ssp membranaceum*) blooms around September. Please do not disturb any plants because they grow slowly and are hard to replace.

Looking east along the Mesa Peak Motorway from the gap in the ridge.

All along the Sespe Formation, particularly in cracks, look for the Santa Susana tarweed (*Hemizonia minthornii*). This tarweed is on California's list of rare plants and although not presently threatened with extinction, is in small numbers throughout the Santa Monica Mountains. You will see more tarweeds on Castro Crest.

Pick your way along the ridge because it is rocky, eroded, and steep in places. At Corral Canyon Road a large parking lot is established as a major trailhead along the Backbone Trail. Depending upon your planning, this could be your destination for the day or a turnaround point. The distance from Piuma Trailhead to Corral Canyon is about 5.3 miles with an elevation gain of 2100 feet. To continue from this point to the next trailhead (on Latigo Canyon Road) is an additional 3.6 miles.

Neither Corral Canyon or Latigo Canyon trailheads have any facilities other than parking.

Backbone Trail along the Sespe formation, heading west to the Corral Canyon Road Trailhead.

PIUMA TRAILHEAD TO CORRAL CANYON TRAILHEAD
and Latigo Canyon Road via Mesa Peak Motorway

	Westbound Miles	Eastbound Miles	
		from Corral Cyn Rd	from Latigo Cyn Rd
Piuma Trailhead	0.00	5.30	8.95
Road to sewage plant (gated)	0.65	4.65	8.30
Puerco M/W east junction	2.50	2.80	6.45
Puerco M/W west junction	2.55	2.75	6.40
Trail to Peak 2049	2.70	2.60	6.25
Ridge Trail on right	4.85	.45	4.10
Corral Canyon Road	5.30	0.00	3.65
Bulldog Motorway	6.10		2.85
Junction with Newton Motorway	6.70		2.25
Trail to Latigo Canyon Road (right turn onto trail)	7.50		1.45
Streambed crossing in upper Newton Canyon	8.45		0.50
Latigo Canyon Road	8.95		0.00

PIUMA TRAILHEAD TO CORRAL CANYON TRAILHEAD
and Latigo Canyon Road via Mesa Peak Motorway

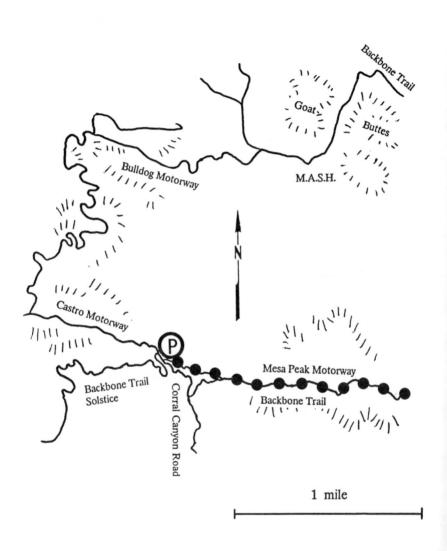

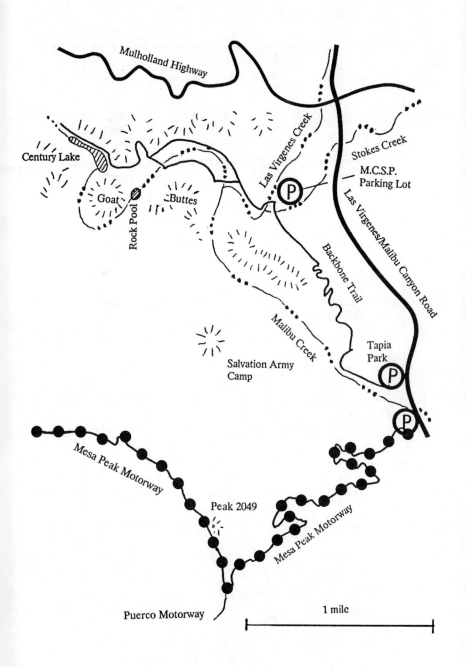

Mulholland Highway

Century Lake

Goat

Rock Pool

Buttes

Las Virgenes Creek

Stokes Creek

M.C.S.P. Parking Lot

Las Virgenes/Malibu Canyon Road

Backbone Trail

Malibu Creek

Salvation Army Camp

Tapia Park

Mesa Peak Motorway

Peak 2049

Mesa Peak Motorway

Puerco Motorway

1 mile

111

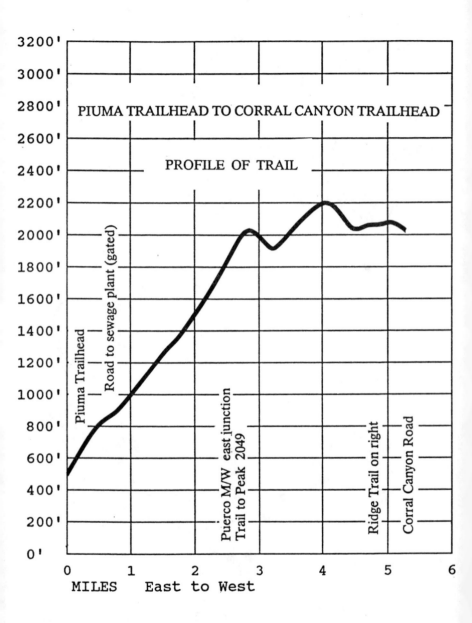

PIUMA TRAILHEAD TO CORRAL CANYON TRAILHEAD

PROFILE OF TRAIL

MILES   East to West

CORRAL CANYON ROAD TO
LATIGO CANYON ROAD

We have an option of continuing another 3.65 miles to Latigo Canyon Road as an extension of the route previously described, or we may make separate trips. We have a further option of going west from Corral Canyon on Backbone Trail/Castro, or Backbone Trail/Solstice. Backbone Trail/Castro goes on the motorway along the crest. Backbone Trail/Solstice is a trail through upper Solstice Canyon. They rejoin on Newton motorway to continue west into Newton Canyon. Using the Castro M/W route the distance is 3.65 miles. Using the Solstice trail the distance is 4.15 miles. Both distances are Corral Canyon Road parking lot to Latigo Canyon Road Parking Lot. I'll describe this option as a loop trip. Either way, you are on the Backbone Trail. I like a counter clockwise route because it takes me high on the ridge for an early overview of canyons on both sides. Also it seems to me that the climb up to Castro ridge after climbing out of Solstice is a lot of elevation gain in one fell swoop. Either way is great, however.

Leave the Corral Canyon parking lot by going uphill on the motorway. Again you will be walking on the Sespe Formation of sandstone, pebbly sandstone, mudstone, and cobbles. Botanists visit here to see Hawkweed, Chaparral Pea, Silver Lotus, Wright's Buckwheat, and Santa Susana Tarweed. These plants thrive on poor, rocky soil and are seldom seen in other parts of the Santa Monica Mountains. Rock formations on both sides are steep, sometimes giving one a feeling of being in a corridor, only to open up to "windows" as we walk along. The view of the canyons below from high on this ridge is striking. Even though muscles may ache from the climb, savor the moment.

In less than one mile on the right, Bulldog motorway comes up from Malibu Creek State Park. About .6 of a mile farther along, at the first motorway on the left, turn onto Newton motorway. You are within 100 feet of being at the highest elevation for the day. A small grove of coast live oaks allows some shade or a lunch spot.

Continue west, downhill for .75 mile and look sharply for a trail on the right going into upper Newton Canyon. At the same place look for the trail coming up from Solstice Canyon on the left.

If you were to continue west on the Backbone Trail you would follow the trail into Newton Canyon and after 1.5 miles arrive at the Latigo Canyon Trailhead.

However, to complete a loop trip back to Corral Canyon, turn left and start downhill on a trail. This area burned completely during the Dayton Canyon fire of October 1982. For a couple of years wildflowers dominated all of upper Solstice Canyon, but as the chaparral regains its previous foothold we will see flowers but not the fields of them that were blooming here in 1983.

The trail picks up Solstice Creek following it down to its confluence with a stream coming from the east. The trail follows up this stream, leaving it to gain more altitude then heads east to the parking area.

The loop is a total of 4.85 miles; 2.2 miles on Backbone Trail/Castro, and 2.65 miles of trail on Backbone Trail/Solstice.

Looking east along Castro Motorway

BACKBONE TRAIL/CASTRO
BACKBONE TRAIL/SOLSTICE
and Newton Canyon Trail

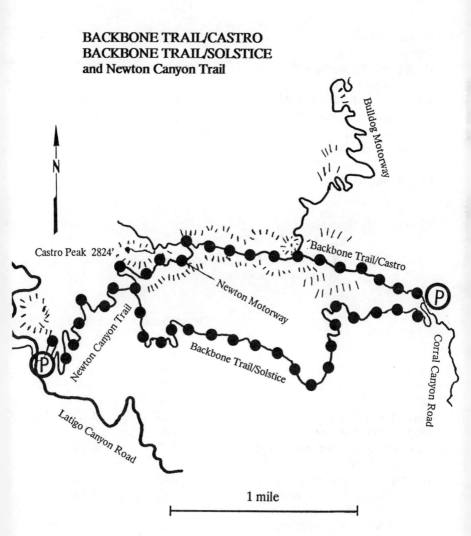

1 mile

CORRAL CANYON ROAD to LATIGO CANYON ROAD
via Castro Motorway

	Westbound Miles	Eastbound Miles
Corral Canyon	0.00	3.65
Bulldog Motorway	.80	2.85
Rock pinnacles north and south of route	1.00	2.65
Junction with Newton M/W	1.40	2.25
Trail to Latigo Canyon Road (right turn onto trail)	2.20	1.45
Streambed crossing in upper Newton Canyon	3.15	.50
Latigo Canyon Road	3.65	0.00

CORRAL CANYON ROAD to LATIGO CANYON ROAD
via upper Solstice Canyon

	Westbound Miles	Eastbound Miles
Corral Canyon Road	0.00	4.15
Service road crossing	.55	3.60
Dry waterfall	.80	3.35
Fork in trail & stream	1.25	2.90
Sloping meadow south of trail	1.40	2.75
Cross stream at lower end of switchbacks	2.05	2.10
Junction with Newton M/W	2.65	1.50
Trail to Latigo Canyon Road (left turn onto trail)	2.70	1.45
Streambed crossing in upper Newton Canyon	3.65	.50
Latigo Canyon Road	4.15	0.00

LATIGO CANYON ROAD TO
KANAN DUME ROAD

This section of the Backbone Trail is closed to public use. Acquisition of land at the western end has not been completed. The western half mile of trail has not been constructed. The information on this trail is for future planning only.

The trail begins on the west side of Latigo Canyon Road opposite the parking lot, and curves right losing altitude. When you reach the "Trail Closed" sign, turn around and come back to the trailhead. When the trail is opened we can expect that the National Park Service will place a trail sign near the trailhead.

When the trail is open for use you can head west, down a ridge to a big switchback to the left. At a streambed the trail switches right and stays on the north-facing slope. Much of the plant community is chaparral giving way to oak woodlands as we progress west. Side streams come down the steep slope allowing the trail entry into shaded glens. Deer are frequently seen on the ridge south of the trail, so look for them.

The trail is on National Park Service land until nearly one-half mile from the western end. An easement has been granted for part of the trail, but not all of it. Privately owned property needs to be acquired before the trail can be completed.

LATIGO CANYON ROAD to KANAN DUME ROAD

	Westbound Miles	Eastbound Miles
Latigo Canyon Road	0.00	2.30
USDI survey marker	.30	2.00
Trail crosses paved driveway	1.80	.50
Gate west of houses	1.90	.40
Ridge above tunnel on Kanan Dume Road	2.05	.25
Parking area on Kanan Dume Road	2.30	0.00

117

Newton Creek

Latigo Road

P

P

TRAIL CLOSED

Kanan Road

1 mile

118

KANAN ROAD TO UPPER TRANCAS CANYON TRAILHEAD

The Backbone Trail has not been built through Zuma and Trancas Canyons. Most of the property is National Park Service land, some is private. Some important properties need be acquired for this 6.5-mile trail corridor for it to be a major scenic attraction. However, from my non-professional viewpoint the trail could be built across these canyons on land now available. Some of the construction would be on difficult steep slopes but in most of such places the views from the trail would be dramatic.

The accompanying map is part NPS early planning, and part conjecture on my part. Aware that I won't be responsible for building this trail, it's easy for me to propose the impossible. In at least two places the terrain is very steep and could be a challenge to build. In any event the proposed route on the map is merely to show where a trail might go, and don't blame any of us if it is incorrect. Don't hike this route until a trail is available.

Depending upon how far north the crossing of both canyons takes place, the altitude gain going west should be about 800 feet out of Zuma and 400 feet out of Trancas. Travelling east out of Trancas will be the stiffest climb — about 950 feet if the crossing of Zuma ridge is near the lower north end. If the crossing of Zuma ridge takes place farther south the respective altitude gains could be 300 to 400 feet more.

Near the east end of this trail segment, Newton Creek joins Zuma Creek. Two spectacular waterfalls on Newton Creek are within range of side trips from the parking lot. Big Zuma waterfall also is nearby, maybe 500 yards, but is deep in the canyon and out of view. A mountaineers' route takes those with Class 3 climbing ability to it, but this route is not for us trail hikers. Farther along Zuma Creek, Upper Zuma waterfall is easily visible from parts of the proposed Backbone Trail. In Zuma you can find deer, coyote, turtles, rattlesnakes, and any number of birds. The National Park Service has not built trails or as yet made it accessible for public use, so be advised to wait awhile to take a safer and more comfortable hike into this area.

Trancas Canyon is smaller than Zuma but is every bit as rugged and beautiful. The waterfalls are not as imposing but the

119

challenge to travel is the same. One spot in an oak woodland might make an overnight trail camp at some future time. As with Zuma Canyon, the National Park Service has built no trails or made any changes to the land so again be advised to wait awhile for travel into this area.

Upper Zuma Waterfall

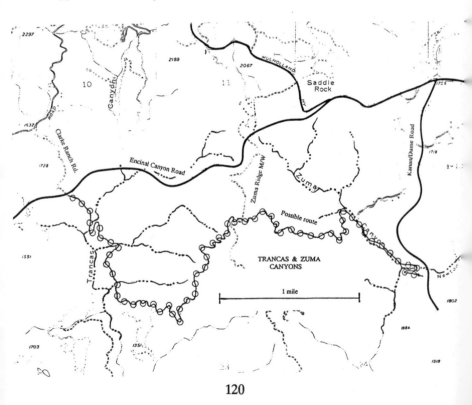

CLARKE RANCH ROAD TO
CIRCLE X RANCH

Clarke Ranch Road begins on the north side of Encinal Canyon Road and goes one-half mile NW to Mulholland Highway. Part of the road crosses NPS property, part crosses private land. Clarke Ranch Road and the NPS property to the west are a logical route for the trail to take.

At this point, however, a public owned trail corridor doesn't exist until near Triunfo Pass along Yerba Buena road. Many of us would like to see the trail go on Etz-Mulloy Motorway, an east-west route high on a ridge. A possible corridor could climb the steep slope joining the motorway about one mile from its east end. Some trails used by local residents do this now. At the west end of the ridge the motorway descends to Yerba Buena Road. The National Park Service owns land on the south side of the road and a trail could be built toward Circle X Ranch paralleling the south side of Yerba Buena Road. Some more land would be required to complete the corridor. Depending upon land acquisition the trailhead would be at East Gate of Circle X, as it now is, or one-half mile east. The map shows a possible route. An elevation gain of 1,100 feet is indicated; a loss of 700 feet is expected. Total distance for this segment should be near 5.5 miles.

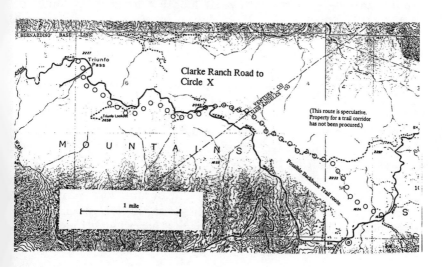

121

CIRCLE X RANCH TO
DANIELSON CAMP

This trail segment crosses the Circle X Ranch east to west and goes down the west ridge of Boney Mountain into Blue Canyon. The upper part of trail on the west ridge has been under construction by a California Conservation Corps crew during 1990, with a couple of miles more before completion. Now, 2.5 miles of Backbone Trail is open through Circle X, and 4 miles is open in Blue Canyon and part way up on the west ridge.

Park in a large lot at the east gate of Circle X Ranch. The parking lot is on Yerba Buena Road 6.5 miles from the Pacific Coast Highway or 4.5 miles from Mulholland Highway. The lot is one mile east of Circle X Ranger Station. (Yerba Buena Road is called Little Sycamore Canyon Road on the east end.)

Go north on a steep, rocky road as it climbs the east facing slope of Sandstone Peak. At .25 mile notice a trail on the right, now called Mishe Mokwa Trail. Off and on it has also been called Split Rock Trail. It joins a trail which originates farther east near Triunfo Pass and goes to Split Rock and up Carlisle Canyon. In 1954 when the Exchange Club bought the backcountry, this trail was called Bedsprings Trail. The road we are on is multi-use for hikers, bicyclists, and equestrians. It continues uphill, gaining nearly 1000 feet in one mile. At the high point look left for a steep route to the top of Sandstone Peak. If you intend to reach the highest point in the Santa Monica Mountains at 3111 feet, a trail on the left begins 150 yards farther west of the high point on the road. This trail is rocky and difficult but a better choice than climbing from the high point on the road. On top notice that Sandstone Peak is an immense volcanic intrusion. The higher elevations of Boney Mountain are volcanic, not a grain of sandstone in sight. Also notice a bronze plaque atop the peak proclaiming it to be Mt. Allen. The Exchange Club, a Los Angeles service organization established the Circle X Ranch in 1949. W. Herbert Allen was a member who totally devoted himself to the project of obtaining property and making it into a camp for accredited youth organizations. In 1965 a movement began to rename Sandstone Peak to Mt. Allen. The Department of Interior has a long standing policy not to approve a geographic name which would honor a living person. Sandstone Peak was not renamed.   Undaunted, on 23 August 1969, an overflow assembly of people gathered atop "Mt. Allen" for the formal dedication.   Hundreds were on the road below and heard the ceremony by walkie-talkie.   Sandstone Peak is Mt. Allen to a segment of the hiking community.

Back on the road, continue west passing Inspiration Point, and as you near two water tanks the trail angles right and goes downhill to the Backcountry Camp.   Here the Backbone Trail forks left and heads westerly.   Not directly because the trail winds around several small peaks, changing direction frequently.   This part of the trail is being built as this book goes to press and from this point on is not open to use.

The next section, not more than 2 miles, has been flagged but not built.   The trail goes through dense chaparral high on the mountain and when it reaches the west ridge going downhill, the vegetation thins out somewhat.   Near Split Rock (on the Boney Mountain range we call three different rocks "Split Rock") the trail begins again and continues down to Danielson Camp.

The Backbone Trail going east up the west ridge.

123

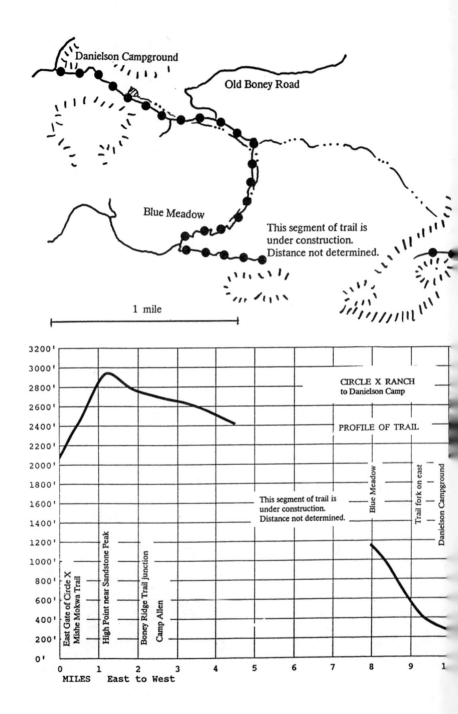

Danielson Campground

Old Boney Road

Blue Meadow

This segment of trail is
under construction.
Distance not determined.

1 mile

CIRCLE X RANCH
to Danielson Camp

PROFILE OF TRAIL

This segment of trail is
under construction.
Distance not determined.

3200'
3000'
2800'
2600'
2400'
2200'
2000'
1800'
1600'
1400'
1200'
1000'
800'
600'
400'
200'
0'

0 1 2 3 4 5 6 7 8 9 1
MILES   East to West

East Gate of Circle X
Mishe Mokwa Trail

High Point near Sandstone Peak

Boney Ridge Trail junction

Camp Allen

Blue Meadow

Trail fork on east

Danielson Campground

CIRCLE X RANCH TO DANIELSON CAMP

CIRCLE X RANCH TO DANIELSON CAMP

	Westbound Miles	Eastbound Miles
Circle X East Gate	0.00	
Mishe Mokwa Trail	0.25	
High Point near Sandstone Peak	1.15	
Boney Ridge Trail	2.00	
Camp Allen	2.50	

This segment of trail is under construction.
The distance has not been determined.

Junction with Old Boney Road at Blue Meadows		2.00
Blue Canyon — Old Boney Rd junction		0.90
Danielson Campground		0.00

DANIELSON CAMPGROUND TO
RAY MILLER TRAILHEAD

Leave the group campground at the Danielson Home and all of its conveniences (including a shower) by going west to Big Sycamore Canyon Trail. Turn left and walk southwest about 1.5 miles to the Wood Canyon Trail. Turn right and follow a trail along the streambed of Wood Canyon. An easy walk of 15 minutes in shade takes us to Deer Camp Junction where we find picnic tables, drinking water, garbage cans, and a restroom. Wood Canyon Creek often runs clear and cool in the spring but dries up during summer and fall. Coast Live Oaks dominate the area, with some sycamores in evidence. Deer Camp Junction is a good place for a lunch stop except for one drawback. Upon leaving the area, "Pumphouse Road" immediately and relentlessly goes uphill gaining 700 feet in .75 mile. One should not be subject to that much misery on a full stomach. In the future a trail now receiving sporadic relocation effort, will go west from Big Sycamore Canyon Trail at a point about 500 feet south of the Wood Canyon Junction. This old trail (now closed) has been flagged for construction at a moderate grade somewhat less steep than the Pumphouse Road. During annual Trail days of 1990 two groups of volunteers worked from both ends but much work remains. The map indicates (symbolically) in dots the general route of this trail.

After the steep 700 foot climb, you will reach a saddle in the north-south ridge separating Sycamore Canyon from LaJolla Valley. The Backbone Trail makes a split at this point in order to accommodate equestrians.

The trail in lower La Jolla Canyon is narrow with a steep drop-off. Horses cannot pass each other, or hikers. Because of this the trail is closed to equestrians, and as an alternate route, the Ray Miller Trail — built in 1989 — makes it possible to ride a horse to the western end of the Backbone Trail. I mention all of this at the junction with the Overlook Trail because equestrians should turn left at this point and go south on the Overlook Trail. Hikers have the option of either trail.

I'll describe the La Jolla Valley and canyon trails first: Continue west going downhill from the Overlook Trail junction. In five minutes the trail forks. The left fork will take you to the Ray

Miller Trailhead at the end of the Backbone Trail. Distance is 2.3 miles. The right fork leads you to the overnight campground where you will find restrooms, drinking water, tables, shade, and space to pitch tents. A pond several hundred yards south of the camp is reached by a trail skirting the west and south shores. This "pond" has been dry for several years but should fill when the rainfall cycle changes. We can continue on this trail to join other trails that may be taken to the Ray Miller Trailhead. Take a look at the map to select the route that fits your time and energy schedule. Mileage and profile for this segment is for the route through the grassland in upper La Jolla Valley. This book includes this mileage in the total miles of Backbone Trail length. A shortcut would take 2 miles off the trip.

Upper La Jolla Valley, one-half mile west of the campground, is a large 600-acre natural grassland. Depending upon one's interests it might be worth while to walk one of the trails through this preserve. Used as pastureland since the days of the original Mexican land grant, the native grasses here are making a partial comeback.

The description of the equestrian route from the ridge at the top of the Pumphouse Road follows: The alternate route to the trailhead — and the only way that is suitable or allowed for equestrians — is south on the Overlook Trail. This is a fireroad on the ridge between La Jolla Canyon and Sycamore Canyon. The Trail overlooks both.

Bill Harris measuring trail mileage.

After walking 35 to 40 minutes and having travelled 2 miles, you will make a big sweeping left turn. The Scenic Trail branches right. A sign indicates the way. Scenic Trail contours along the west facing slope of Peak 1132, then comes out on a ridge pointed toward the ocean. La Jolla Canyon and the Ray Miller Trailhead are below and in view to the west. The Ray Miller Trail is quite visible making switchbacks below. One-half mile after turning on to the Scenic Trail look closely for the Ray Miller Trail. The Scenic Trail continues down the ridge and to follow it would take you to Sycamore Canyon. Horses are not allowed in Lower Sycamore Canyon so don't plan to exit there. Turn right onto the Ray Miller Trail. Two miles later you are at the trailhead.

An equestrian staging area is available in La Jolla Canyon 500 feet east of the parking lot at the Ray Miller Trailhead. For overnight parking of vehicles one would want to check with a Point Mugu State Park ranger in advance.

Thornhill Broome Beach from the Ray Miller Trail

128

DANIELSON CAMP TO RAY MILLER TRAILHEAD
via La Jolla Valley Grassland

	Westbound Miles	Eastbound Miles
Danielson Campground	0.00	7.45
Ranch Center Road	0.30	7.15
Wood Canyon Trail	1.55	5.90
Deer Camp Junction	2.25	5.20
Saddle at Overlook Trail	2.95	4.50
Junction with La Jolla Canyon Trail	3.15	4.30
Walk-in Campground	3.35	4.10
Trail to pond	3.55	3.90
Trail on left (east edge of grassland)	3.95	3.50
Trail on left (through grassland)	4.65	2.80
Trail junction near stream	5.45	2.00
Join LaJolla Canyon Trail	6.25	1.20
Waterfall	6.75	0.70
Ray Miller Trailhead	7.45	0.00

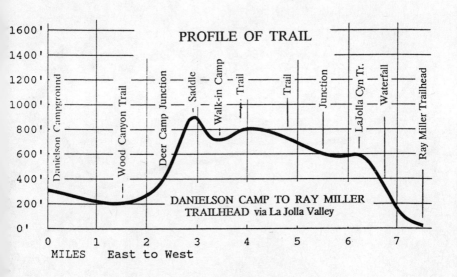

PROFILE OF TRAIL

DANIELSON CAMP TO RAY MILLER TRAILHEAD via La Jolla Valley

MILES   East to West

DANIELSON CAMP TO RAY MILLER TRAILHEAD
via La Jolla Valley Grassland

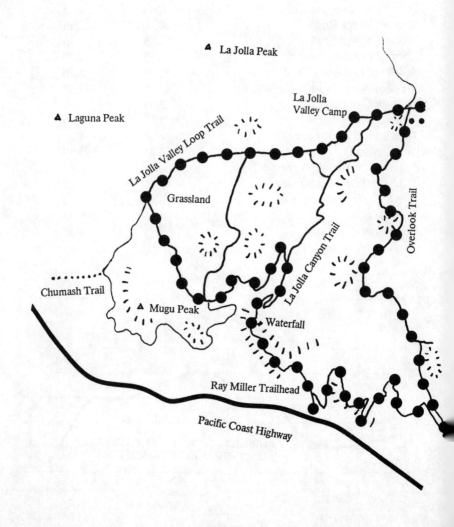

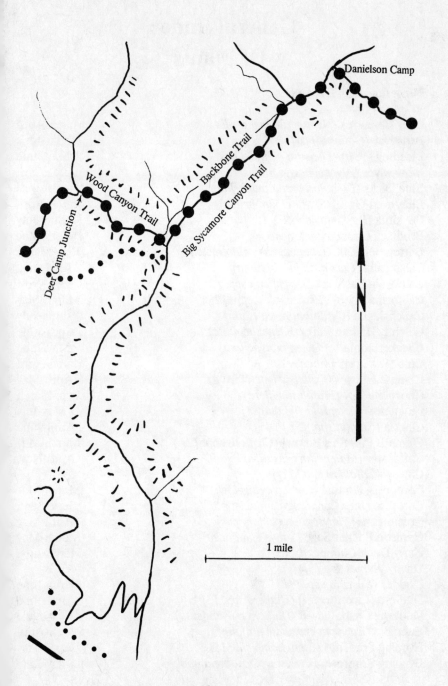

General Index
Of Plants

Flowering and Herbaceous

Baby Blue-eyes *(Nemophila menziesii)*	March-April
Bedstraw *(Galium spp. [3])*	March-June
Bleeding Heart *(Dicentra ochroleuca)*	May-June
Blow-wives *(Achyrachaena mollis)*	April
Blue Dicks *(Dicholostemma pulchellum)*	March-April
Blue-eyed Grass *(Sisyrinchium bellum)*	March-April
Boykinia *(Boykinia spp [2])*	May-July
Brodiaea *(Brodiaea jolonensis)*	April-May
Buttercup, Calif. *(Ranunculus californicus)*	Feb.-March
Calabazilla *(Cucurbita foetidissima)*	June-Aug.
California Fuchsia *(Zauschneria spp. [2])*	Aug.-Nov.
California Poppy *(Eschscholzia spp. [2])*	March-May
Canchalagua *(Centaurium venustum)*	June-July
Catchfly [Indian Pink] *(Silene laciniata)*	April-June
Checkerbloom *(Sidalcea malvaeflora)*	May-June
Chia *(Salvia columbariae)*	March-April
Chinese Houses *(Collinsia heterophylla)*	April-May
Chocolate Lily *(Fritillaria biflora)*	Feb.-March
Cinquefoil *(Potentilla glandulosa)*	May-July
Clarkia *(Clarkia spp. [5])*	April-June
Clematis [Virgin's Bower] *(Clematis spp. [2])*	March-May
Cliff Aster *(Malacothrix saxatilis)*	April-Nov.
Clover *(Trifolium spp.[11])*	
Coreopsis, Annual *(Coreopsis bigelovii)*	March-May
Corethrogyne *(Corethrogyne filaginifolia)*	June-Sept.
Cream-cups *(Platystemon californicus)*	April-May
Crimson Pitcher Sage *(Salvia spathacea)*	March-May
Curly Dock *(Rumex crispus)* *	March-June
Dock *(Rumex spp [3])*	
Dodder *(Cuscuta spp. [4])*	March-June
Dudleya [Live-forever] *(Dudleya spp. [3])*	April-June
Dudleya, Chalk-leaved *(Dudleya pulverulenta)*	August
Eucrypta *(Eucrypta chrysanthemifolia)*	March-April
Evening Primrose *(Camissonia spp. [5])*	April-May
Evening Primrose, Hooker's *(Oenothera hookeri)*	May-June

Everlasting [Cudweed] *(Gnaphalium spp. [7])*	Jan.-Oct.
Fennel *(Foeniculum vulgare)* *	May-July
Fiddleneck *(Amsinckia spp. [2])*	March-May
Fiesta Flower *(Pholistoma auritum)*	March-April
Figwort *(Scrophularia californica)*	March-June
Filaree [Storksbill] *(Erodium spp. [4])**	Feb.-May
Fire Poppy *(Papaver californicum)*	April
Fleabane *(Erigeron foliosus)*	May-June
Four O'clock *(Mirabilis laevis)*	March-June
Gilia *(Gilia spp. [2])*	April-May
Globe Lily *(Calochortus albus)*	April-May
Goldenbush *(Haplopappus spp [4])*	
Goldenrod *(Solidago spp [2])*	Aug.-Nov.
Golden Yarrow *(Eriophyllum confertiflorum)*	April-May
Golden Stars *(Bloomeria crocea)*	April-May
Goldfields *(Lasthenia spp. [2])*	April-May
Gourd *(Cucurbita foetidissima)*	June-July
Ground Pink *(Linanthus dianthiflorus)*	April
Groundsel, Bush *(Senecio douglasii)*	April-May
Groundsel, Common *(Senecio vulgaris)* *	Jan.-May
Gumweed *(Grindelia robusta)*	April-June
Hedge Nettle, Rigid *(Stachys rigida)*	March-Aug.
Hedge Nettle *(Stachys bullata)*	March-May
Hedge Nettle, White *(Stachys albens)*	June-Aug.
Heliotrope *(Heliotropium curassavicum)*	June-Aug.
Hemlock, Poison *(Conium maculatum)* *	May-July
Horehound *(Marrubium vulgare)* *	March-May
Humboldt Lily *(Lilium Humboldtii)*	June-July
Indian Paintbrush *(Castilleja spp. [4])*	March-May
Indian Warrior *(Pedicularis densiflora)*	Feb.-April
Jewel-flower *(Streptanthus heterophyllus)*	March-April
Jimson-weed *(Datura wrightii)*	May-July
Lacepod [Fringepod] *(Thysanocarpus curvipes)*	March-May
Larkspur, Blue *(Delphinium spp. [2])*	March-May
Larkspur, Scarlet *(Delphinium cardinale)*	June-July
Leather Root *(Psoralea macrostachya)*	June-Aug.
Lomatium *(Lomatium spp. [4])*	Jan.-May
Lotus *(Lotus spp. [7])*	March-Aug.
Lupine *(Lupinus spp. [8]*	March-May
Man-root [Wild Cucumber] *(Marah macrocarpus)*	Jan.-April
Mariposa Lily,, Butterfly *(Calachortus venustus)*	May-July
Mariposa Lily, Catalina *(Calochortus catalinae)*	March-April

133

Mariposa Lily, Lilac *(Calachortus splendens)*	May-June
Mariposa Lily, Plummers *(Calochortus plummerae)*	June-July
Mariposa Lily, Yellow *(Calochortus clavatus)*	May
Matilija Poppy *(Romneya coulteri)* *	April-May
Microseris *(Microseris spp [4])*	
Milkmaids *(Cardamine californica)*	Feb.-April
Milkweed, Calif. *(Asclepias californica)*	March-June
Milkweed, Narrowleaf *(Asclepias fascicularis)*	May-Sept.
Miners' Lettuce *(Claytonia perfoliata)*	March-April
Monkeyflower, Bush *(Diplacus longiflorus)*	April-June
Monkeyflower, Common *(Mimulus guttatus)*	March-May
Monkeyflower, Scarlet *(Mimulus cardinalis)*	June-Aug.
Monkeyflower, Slimy *(Mimulus floribundis)*	April-Aug.
Monkeyflower, *Yellow (Mimulus brevipes)*	March-May
Morning Glory *(Calystegia macrostegia)*	Feb.-June
Mountain Dandelion *(Agoseris grandiflora)*	May-June
Mustard, Common *(Brassica campestris)* *	All year
Mustard, Black *(Brassica nigra)* *	March-July
Mustard, Tansy *(Descurainia pinnata)*	March-June
Mustard, Tower *(Arabis glabra)*	March-July
Onion, Wild *(Allium spp. [2])*	March-May
Owl's Clover *(Orthocarpus purpurascens)*	March-May
Pansy [Johnny-Jump-up] *(Viola pedunculata)*	April-May
Pea, Wild Sweet *(Lathyrus laetiflorus)*	Feb.-June
Pennyroyal *(Monardella hypoleuca)*	June-July
Penstemon, Climbing *(Keckiella cordifolia)*	May-July
Penstemon, Foothill *(Penstemon heterophyllus)*	April-June
Penstemon, Showy *(Penstemon spectabilis)*	April-May
Peony *(Paeonia californica)*	Jan.-March
Perezia *(Perezia microcephala)*	June-July
Phacelia, Branching *(Phacelia ramosissima)*	May-July
Phacelia, Caterpillar *(Phacelia cicutaria)*	March-June
Phacelia, Fern-leaf *(Phacelia distans)*	March-June
Phacelia, Large-flowered *(Phacelia grandiflora)*	April-June
Phacelia, Mountain *(Phacelia imbricata)*	April-June
Phacelia, Parry's *(Phacelia parryi)*	March-May
Phacelia, Sticky *(Phacelia viscida)*	April-June
Phacelia, Yellow-throated *(Phacelia brachyloba)*	May-June
Pimpernel *(Anagallis arvensis)* *	March-June
Pincushion, Pink *(Chaenactis artemisiaefolia)*	May-June
Pincushion, Golden *(Chaenactis glabriuscula)*	March-April
Pineapple Weed *(Matricaria matricarioides)*	Feb.-May

Popcorn Flower *(Cryptantha spp. [4])*	March-May
Popcorn Flower *(Plagiobothrys spp. [3])*	March-May
Radish, Wild *(Raphanus sativus)* *	All year
Rattleweed or Locoweed *(Astragalus spp [4])*	
Redmaids *(Calandrinia spp [2])*	Feb.-May
Rock-rose *(Helianthemum scoparium)*	Feb.-May
Sanicle *(Sanicula spp. [4])*	March-May
Saxifrage, Calif. *(Saxifraga californica)*	March-May
Scarlet Bugler *(Penstemon centranthifolius)*	April-May
Shooting Stars *(Dodecatheon clevelandii)*	Jan.-March
Skullcap *(Scutellaria tuberosa)*	March-April
Snapdragon, Rose *(Antirrhinum multiflorum)*	May-June
Snapdragon, Twining *(Antirrhinum kelloggii)*	March-April
Snapdragon, Violet *(Antirrhinum nuttallianum)*	April-May
Snapdragon, White *(Antirrhinum coulterianum)*	April-May
Soap Plant *(Chlorogalum pomeridianum)*	May-June
Sow Thistle *(Sonchus spp.)* *	All year
Stream Orchid *(Epipactis gigantea)*	May-June
Sunflower, Canyon *(Venegasia carpesioides)*	March-May
Sunflower, Bush [Shrub] *(Encelia californica)*	March-June
Sunflower, Prairie *(Helianthus annuus)* *	April-Sept.
Sunflower, Slender *(Helianthus gracilentus)*	April-Sept.
Sweet Clover *(Melilotus spp. [2])*	March-June
Tarweed *(Hemizonia spp. [2])*	April-June
Tarweed *(Madia spp. [3])*	April-June
Tauschia *(Tauschia spp [2])*	Feb.-June
Telegraph Weed *(Heterotheca grandiflora)*	June-Aug.
Thistle, Calif. *(Cirsium californicum)*	April-June
Thistle, Bull *(Cirsium vulgare)* *	June-Oct.
Thistle, Milk *(Silybum marianum)* *	May-July
Thistle, Star *(Centaurea melitensis)* *	May-July
Thistle, Western *(Cirsium coulteri)*	March-June
Thistle, Yellow Star *(Centaurea spp [2])**	
Tidy Tips *(Layia platyglossa)*	March-May
Turkish Rugging *(Chorizanthe staticoides)*	April-June
Verbena *(Verbena lasiostachys)*	April-Sept.
Verbena, Beach *(Abronia spp. [2])*	April-June
Vetch *(Vicia spp. [3])*	March-May
Vinegar Weed *(Trichostema lanceolatum)*	May-June
Wallflower *(Erysimum spp. [2])*	March-May
Whispering Bells *(Emmenanthe penduliflora)*	March-May
Windmill Pink *(Silene gallica)**	Feb.-June

Woodland Star *(Lithophragma affine)*	April-May
Woolly Aster *(Corethrogyne filaginifolia)*	June-Sept.
Yarrow [White] *(Achillea borealis)*	May-June
Zygadene [Star Lily] *(Zygadenus fremontii)*	March-April

* alien (non-native) plants

This list of annuals and perennial flowering plants is not meant to be complete. Their abundance or rarity each year is related not only to habitat and seasonal weather variations, but also to the periodic occurrence of fire. Almost all of the listed plants produce an abundance of bloom the first season after fire that is way beyond the normal; some of them only bloom after a fire.

Trees

Alder, White *(Alnus rhombifolia)*
Ash (Fraxinus spp [2])
Cottonwood *(Populus spp [2])*
Laurel [Bay] *(Umbellularia californica)*
Maple, Bigleaf *(Acer macrophylla)*
Oak, Coast Live *(Quercus agrifolia)*
Oak, Valley *(Quercus lobata)*
Sycamore *(Platanus racemosa)*
Walnut, Calif. *(Juglans californica)*

Shrubs
RIDGES AND HIGHER SLOPES

Bricklebush *(Brickellia spp. [2])*	Sept.-Nov.
Buckwheat, Calif. *(Eriogonum fasciculatum)*	April-July
Buckwheat, Ashyleaf *(Eriogonum cinereum)*	June-Sept.
Buckwheat, Conejo *(Eriogonum crocatum)*	May-June
Buckwheat, Longstem *(Eriogonum elongatum)*	Aug.-Oct.
Bush Sunflower *(Encelia californica)*	March-June
Chaparral Pea *(Pickeringia montana)*	April-May
Ceanothus, Bigpod *(Ceanothus megacarpus)*	Feb.-April
Ceanothus, Buckbrush *(Ceanothus cuneatus)*	Feb.-April
Ceanothus, Greenbark *(Ceanothus spinosus)*	March-May
Ceanothus, Hairyleaf *(Ceanothus oliganthus)*	March-April
Ceanothus, Hoaryleaf *(Ceanothus crassifolius)*	March-April

Ceanothus, Whitethorn *(Ceanothus leucodermis)*	April-June
Chamise *(Adenostoma fasciculatum)*	May-June
Cherry, Hollyleaf *(Prunus ilicifolia)*	April-May
Coyote Brush *(Baccharis pilularia)*	Aug.-Nov.
Deerweed *(Lotus scoparius)*	March-June
Goldenbush *(Haplopappus spp. [4])*	Sept.-Oct.
Laurel Sumac *(Rhus Laurina)*	May-June
Mallow, Bush *(Malacothamnus fasciculatus)*	May-Oct.
Manzanita, Bigberry *(Arctostaphylos glauca)*	Jan.-March
Manzanita, Eastwood *(Arctostaphylos glandulosa)*	Jan.-March
Mountain Mahogany *(Cercocarpus betuloides)*	March-May
Poppy, Bush or Tree *(Dendromecon rigida)*	Feb.-May
Prickly Phlox *(Leptodactylon californicum)*	Jan.-April
Rattleweed [Locoweed] *(Astragalus spp. [5])*	March-June
Redberry *(Rhamnus crocea)*	January-April
Redberry, Hollyleaf *(Rhamnus ilicifolia)*	Feb.-April
Redshanks *(Adenostoma sparsifolium)*	August
Sage, Black *(Salvia mellifera)*	April-June
Sage, Purple *(Salvia leucophylla)*	May-July
Sage, White *(Salvia apiana)*	April-June
Sagebrush, Coastal *(Artemesia californica)*	Aug.-Oct.
Scrub Oak *(Quercus dumosa)*	March-April
Silk Tassel *(Garrya veatchii)*	Jan.-March
Squaw Bush *(Rhus trilobata)*	March-April
Sugar Bush *(Rhus ovata)*	March-May
Toyon *(Heteromeles arbutifolia)*	May-June
Woolly Blue-curls *(Trichostema lanatum)*	April-June
Yerba Santa *(Eriodictyon crassifolium)*	April-May
Yucca *(Yucca whipplei)*	May-June

Shrubs

STREAMSIDE

Blackberry *(Rubus ursinus)*	March-April
Cat-tail *(Typha latifolia)*	Aug.-Oct.
Mugwort *(Artemesia douglasiana)*	July-Nov.
Mulefat *(Baccharis viminea)*	Jan.-May
Nettle, Dwarf *(Urtica urens)*	Jan.-April
Willow *(Salix spp. [3])*	Jan.-March

OCEAN FACING

Coreopsis *(Coreopsis gigantea)*	March-May
Lemonadeberry *(Rhus integrifolia)*	Feb.-April
Prickly Pear *(Opuntia littoralis)*	May-June
Saltbush *(Atriplex lentiformis)*	July-Oct.

CANYONS AND LOWER SLOPES

Castor-bean *(Ricinus communis)* *	All year
Cinquefoil *(Potentilla glandulosa)*	April-June
Coffeeberry, Calif. *(Rhamnus californica)*	May-June
Currant, Chaparral *(Ribes malvaceum)*	Dec.-Feb.
Currant, Golden *(Ribes aureum)*	March-April
Elderberry *(Sambucus mexicana)*	April-Aug.
Gooseberry, Fuchsia-flowered *(Ribes speciosum)*	Jan.-March
Honeysuckle *(Lonicera subspicata)*	May-July
Lupine, Pauma *(Lupinus longiflorus)*	April-June
Nightshade, Black *(Solanum douglasii)*	All year
Nightshade, Purple *(Solanum xantii)*	Jan.-Aug.
Ocean Spray [Creambush]*(Holodiscus discolor)*	April-May
Poison Oak *(Toxicodendron diversilobum)* (old name: *Rhus diversiloba)*	Feb.-March
Rose, Calif. Wild *(Rosa californica)*	April-May
Snowberry *(Symphoricarpos mollis)*	April-May
Spanish Broom *(Spartium junceum)* *	April-June
Tobacco, Tree or Bush *(Nicotiana glauca)* *	All year

* Denotes alien (non-native) plant

The list of shrubs and trees for the Santa Monica Mountains is not complete. There are some rarely found plants that are not included because of space limitations. The division of shrubs according to habitat is not meant to be taken literally; there is much overlapping of species in the areas listed. Blooming months are also meant only as a guideline; there can be variations related to both the particular year's weather and the individual habitat.

The information in this index has been compiled by James P. Kenney.

NON-FLOWERING PLANTS AND GRASSES

Birdsfoot Fern *(Pellaea mucronata)*
Bracken Fern, Western *(Pteridium aquilinum)*
Chain Fern, Giant *(Woodwardia fimbriata)*
Coffee Fern *(Pellaea andromedifolia)*
Giant Rye *(Elymus spp.)*
Goldback Fern *(Pityrogramma triangularis)*
Horsetail *(Equisetum spp.)*
Maidenhair Fern *(Adiantum spp.)*
Woodfern, Coastal *(Dryopteris arguta)*

General Index
Of Animals

AMPHIBIANS
Arboreal Salamander *(Aneides lugubris)*
Arroyo Toad *(Bufo microscaphus)*
Bullfrog *(Rana catesbeiana)*..an introduced frog
California Newt *(Taricha torosa torosa)*
California Slender Salamander *(Batrachoseps attenuatus)*
California Treefrog *(Hyla cadaverina)* Ensatina or Eschscholtz's
Salamander *(Ensatina eschscholtzi)*
Garden Slender Salamander *(Batrachoseps major)*
Pacific Treefrog *(Hyla regilla)*
Western Spadefoot *(Scaphiopus hammondi)*
Western Toad *(Bufo boreas)*

BIRDS
Acorn Woodpecker *(Melanerpes formicivorus)*
Allen's Hummingbird *(Selasphorus sasin)*
Anna's Hummingbird *(Calypte anna)*
Barn Owl *(Tyto alba)*
Barn Swallow *(Hirundo rustica)*
Bewick's Wren *(Thryomanes bewickii)*
Black-chinned Hummingbird *(Archilochus alexandri)*
Black-crowned Night Heron *(Nycticorax nycticorax)*
Black-headed Grosbeak *(Pheucticus melanocephalus)*
Black-throated grey warbler *(Dendroica nigrescens)*
Bluebird *(Sialia mexicana)*
Brown Towhee *(Pipilo fuscus)*
Bushtit *(Psaltriparus minimus)*
California Quail *(Lophortyx californicus)*
California Thrasher *(Toxostoma redivivum)*
Coot *(Fulica americana)*
Dark-eyed "Oregon" Junco *(Junco hyemalis)*
Ducks - various migratory:
  Pintail *(Anas jamaicensis)*
  Ruddyduck *(Oxyura jamaicensis)*
  Shoveler *(Anas clypeata)*

140

Green-winged teal *(Anas crecca)* winter
Cinnamon teal *(Anas cyanoptera)* summer
Golden Eagle *(Aquila chrysaetos)*
Goldfinch, Lawrencis *(Carduelis lawrencei)*
Great Blue Heron *(Ardea herodias)*
Great Horned Owl *(Bubo virginianus)*
House Finch *(Carpodacus mexicanus)*
Kingfisher *(Megaceryle alcyon)*
Lark Sparrow *(Chondestes grammacus)*
Lesser Goldfinch *(Carduelis psaltria)*
Loggerhead Shrike *(Lanius ludevicianus)*
Mallard Duck *(Anas platyrhynchos)*
Mourning Dove *(Zenaida macroura)*
Nuttail's Woodpecker *(Picoides nuttallii)*
Phainopepla *(Phainopepla nitens)*
*Plain Titmouse (Parus in*ornatus)
Raven *(Corvus corax)*
Red-shouldered Hawk *(Buteo lineatus)*
Redtail Hawk *(Buteo jamaicensis)*
Redwing Blackbird *(Agelaius phoeniceus)*
Rough-winged Swallow *(Stelgidopteryx ruficollis)*
Rufus-sided Towhee *(Pipilo erythropthalmus)*
Scrub Jay *(Aphelocoma coerulescens)*
Song Sparrow *(Melospiza melodia)*
Turkey Vulture *(Cathartes aura)* Buzzard
Western Tanager *(Piranga ludoviciana)*
White-breasted Nuthatch *(Sitta carolinensis)*
White-crowned Sparrow *(Zenotrichia leucophrys)*
Wood Peewee *(Contopus sordidulus)*
Wrentit *(Chamaea fasciata)*

Technical names of birds correspond with those found in the Audubon Society Field Guide to North American Birds - Western Region.

MAMMALS
Bat *(various species)*
Bush Rabbit *(Sylvilagus bachmanii)*
Black-tailed Jackrabbit (Lepus Californicum)
California Mule Deer *(Odocoileus hemionus)*
Cottontail Rabbit *(Sylvilagus audubonii)*
Coyote *(Canis latrans)*

Deer Mouse *(Peromyscus maniculatus)* White-footed
Feral Domestic Cat *(Felis domesticus)*
Gray Fox *(Urocyon cinoreoargenteus)*
Gray Whale *(Cochruchtius robustus)*
Ground Squirrel *(Otospermophilus beacheyii)*
Kangaroo Rat *(Dipodomys Sp.)*
Long-tailed Weasel *(Mustela frenata)*
Meadow Mouse *(Microtus californicus)*
Mole
Mountain Lion *(Felis concolor)*
Pocket Gopher *(Thommys bottae)*
Raccoon *(Procyon lotor)*
Ring-tailed Cat *(Bassariscus natantus)* ?
Shrew
Striped Skunk *(Mephitis mephitis)*
Western Gray Squirrel *(Scinrus griseus)* ?
Wild Cat
Woodrat *(Neotoma sp.)*

REPTILES

California Legless Lizard *(Anniella pulchra)*
California Mountain Kingsnake *(L. Zonata)*
California Striped Whipsnake *(Masticophis lateralis)*
Coachwhip [Red Racer] *(Masticophis flagellum)*
Coast Horned Lizard *(Phrynosoma coronatum)*
Common Kingsnake *(Lampropeltis getulus)*
Gilberts Skink *(Eumeces gilberti)*
Gopher Snake *(Pituophis melanoleucus)*
Night Snake *(Hypsiglena torquata)*
Racer *(Coluber constrictor)*
Ringneck Snake *(Diadophis punctatus)*
Side-blotched Lizard *(Uta stansburiana)*
Southern Alligator Lizard *(Gerrhonotus multicarinatus)*
Southern Pacific Rattlesnake *(Crotalus viridis)*
Striped Racer *(Masticophis lateralis)*
Western Aquatic Garter Snake or Two Striped Garter
   Snake *(Thamnophis couchi hammondi)*
Western Fence Lizard *(Scelooporus occidentalis)*
Western Pond Turtle *(Clemmys marmorata)*
Western Skink *(Eumeaces skiltonianus)*
Western Whiptail *(Cnemidophorus tigris)*

Epilogue

In the area in which we live, the demand for land is great. Open space, parks, and trails no longer happen by accident. Only through our efforts now, will we set aside recreational areas. Most of us think of leaving a heritage for our children, or grandchildren. A fine legacy, but we must look further into the future and think of hundreds — even thousands — of generations to come. The future will be sad without relict communities where people can be with nature.

Part of my reason for writing this book is to make it attractive now, for more people to see this land. To be in the Santa Monica Mountains is to become passionate about their preservation.

For many years we have seen a growing concern for the future. A great many of our elected and appointed representatives in all levels of government have worked toward the use of open space as an improvement to the cultural and intellectual development of the Nation. Millions of us at the grass roots level are making our needs and desires known. Through foresight, a strong will, and the development of a proper political climate, we will succeed — not for ourselves — but for the future.